ANOTHER TIME – ANOTHER PLACE

Recollections of the past

Published by the Bay Owl Press, 2023
an imprint of the Perera-Hussein Publishing House
www.pererahussein.com

Copyright © Anthea Senaratna
First Edition

ISBN: 978-624-5831-01-2

All rights reserved

Another Time – Another Place: Recollections of the Past is a personal memoir. The right of Anthea Senaratna to be identified as the Author of this work has been asserted by her in accordance with the Copyright, Designs & Patents Act.

Printed and bound by Thomson Press

 To offset the environmental pollution caused by printing books, the Perera-Hussein Publishing House grows trees in Puttalam, Sri Lanka's semi-arid zone.

ANOTHER TIME – ANOTHER PLACE

Recollections of the past

Anthea Senaratna

ALSO BY
ANTHEA SENARATNA

Dancing with the Dogs and other short stories
The Mango Tree – stories & sketches
A Flash of Red and other stories

This book is dedicated to my children Sonali and Dimitri and grandchildren Akash, Audrey and Isaak – and the future generations!

PART ONE

A SHORT HISTORY OF MY FAMILY

Mother

My mother was Audrey Miriam Meynert Herft (born 18th February 1903, died 2nd January 1963).

My mother's father Cecil Richard Lorensz Herft was an Engineer in the Public Works Department of the Western and North-Western Province. He was born in 1860 in Mannar and married Lilian Meynert – also born in Mannar. They lived in Negombo in a large house named Ripplehurst which is now the Kudapadu Police Station in Negombo. The HERFT family was a distinguished family of NEGOMBO. C. R. L. Herft was involved with the inauguration of NEWSTEAD COLLEGE, Negombo, a very well-known school even to this day! He, along with St John Pereira, a Negombo resident, was responsible for the erection of the Bells of St Mary's in Negombo.

When they moved to Colombo they lived in a house at the top of Charlemont Road facing the Galle Road called Agincourt. It stood opposite to where the Savoy Cinema is currently located.

Cecil and Lilian had several children – 6 daughters and 5 sons.

*They were – Doreen Meynert (1898), Chapman Lorensz (1899), Cecil Eldred (1900), Idona Elspeth (1900), Lorenza Neomi (Oct 11 1901), **Audrey Miriam** (1903),*

Thelma Lilian (1904), Esme Bertha Susanna (1908), Swinburne Annesley (1910)Fenton Vyville (1911), & Orville Wesley (1914).

My Mother's siblings whom I recall were – **Cecil Eldred** – we called him Uncle Eldie, **Annesley, Vyville** and **Orville** and the aunts were **Idone Elspeth** – we called her **Auntie Dona, Esme,** and **Thelma.**

Father

My father was Frederick Ernest Jansz (born 1st June 1901 died 8th June 1978).

My father's parents were James Collingwood Jansz (born 2nd May 1862). He married Charlotte Henrietta Heyn. My grandfather James Collingwood Jansz had a very interesting profession – he was a teacher of English, Latin and Greek at Royal College Colombo and was also the founder President of the Young Men's Christian Association movement in Ceylon in 1882.

They had eleven children – five boys and six girls – though some of them died at a very young age.

Estelle Ray (1884). Phyllida Florence (1885), Queenie Hester (1887), Rachel Henrietta (1889), James Collingwood Renny (1890), Zillah Claribel (1892), Rupert Heyn (1894) & the twins Thomas Hugh and Rupert Heyn (1894). Neville Bertram (1895), Rizpah Mirandah (1897), **Frederick Ernest (1901).**

My Father's siblings whom I recall were **Phyllida** (we called her Aunty Phylla), **Queenie, Rachel, Zillah, Hugh,** and **Neville.**

It was typical for families at that time to have at least ten to twelve children – an unbelievable idea today! Both my parents had several siblings and it was also not unusual for the children to die of pneumonia, tuberculosis, malaria and other common illnesses. So many of my parents' family members died in this way – some when they were babies and others slightly older. Perhaps this is why families were large so that when four or five died there were always at least six or seven to carry on the family name!

I don't really know where I should begin. Perhaps I should try to do so from the beginning; the beginning of what I can remember that is – for the beginning of me does not seem to exist even though it did!

I was born on the 30th June 1944, in the city of Kandy, the hill capital, one-time home of the great Kandyan kings of Sri Lanka. This was a kingdom once, unattainable by foreigners until, after years of endeavour the British came and, after much crafty negotiation signed a treaty with the Kandyan Chieftains permitting them to control the Kingdom of Kandy while they – the British would control the rest of the island. It is a matter of history that a short time after the agreement was signed the British did not keep to their side of the treaty and betrayed the Kandyan chieftains by taking control of the entire island. When this happened, the entire country was in the hands of a foreign power.

My family resided in Kandy and I was born at the tail end of the Second World War. But none of this do I remember. Naturally! My sister Lorna (later called Lorni) would have been eight years old and my brother (James Cecil) called Jim, 11 years when I was born. My sister tells me that she well recalls the day I was born☺. Babies were generally born at home with the aid of a midwife. Only if complications arose did pregnant mothers go to the hospital for child-birth. So, the day had come and my mother was telling the household helpers (two of them I gather) to get some boiling water organised for the birth – they were rushing from room to room trying to get a suitable container for the water. Lorni was totally bewildered by all this calamity and didn't know for what on earth they needed boiling water. When she asked one of the helpers, she got the answer that it was for the birth of the baby (which was going to be me!) My sister being just eight of course thought they were going to put me, the new born baby, into boiling water! She screamed and cried and then my mother with all her labour pains and whatever else had to explain that it was not meant to boil the baby but to sterilise any instruments which may be needed by the midwife in the delivery. Oh gosh what a relief for Lorni! Anyway, ultimately my dad got an ambulance and took my mother to the Civil Hospital in Kandy where I was born.

My sister tells me that my dad, who was a Government servant, was transferred to Badulla and we lived there for about two years. I was just a baby then. My brother and sister (and myself too) were prone to catching malaria ever so often. We would go into shivering fits and record soaring temperatures and had to be given ice baths to bring the fever down. Because of this happening very regularly my parents decided to send my brother and sister (who must have been around twelve and nine years respectively) to schools in Colombo where they would stay with my father's sisters who occupied a large house down Castle Street – my brother attended Wesley College and my sister Presbyterian Girls' School, Regent Street. I too became familiar with this house in later years.

During World War II, Ceylon, as our country was called at that time, served as a British base against the Japanese. Ceylon in fact became a vital feature in the British Empire with Lord Louis Mountbatten using Peradeniya as his headquarters for the Eastern Theater (the South –East Asian Theatre was the name given to the campaigns of the Pacific War in Burma, Ceylon, India, Thailand, Indochina, Malaya and Singapore). The idea in conquering these countries was to seize control of the natural resources such as rubber from the European colonies in this region. It was in 1942 that the Japanese bombed Ceylon. However, with the bombings of Hiroshima and Nagasaki by the United States of America, the Second World War was finally brought to a close in the 'official' sense.

During this period my father was once again transferred (I reckon Government servants were transferred every two years or so). From what I can recall he was posted to Matara (in the south of the country) but my mother stayed in Colombo. This was because my brother and sister attended schools in Colombo and I of course had to stay with my mother. I must have been around three or four years old at the time and it is actually at this point in time that my memory catches up with the happenings in my life.

We lived in a spacious two-storeyed house called *Smyrna* at the lower end of Mount Mary, Karlshrue Gardens, at Borella. (Incidentally the name Smyrna was the name of one of the seven churches mentioned in the Book of Revelation in the Bible). My family consisting of my parents, my brother Jim, sister Lorni myself and of course our dog – an English Sheepdog – Kim, lived downstairs. The upstairs section was occupied by Walter and Myrtle de Silva. I remember well their big sturdy dog Nero. The de Silvas were wonderful – more family than tenants. I was constantly dashing upstairs and playing on their large wide open to the skies balcony. I remember how we couldn't keep food on our dining table because Nero would help himself to it! I was always amazed at the way he just placed his front paws on the table and slurped up the soup straight from the bowl! Downstairs in an extra room we had Egerton Batuwitage – we used to call him Batu, and I recall he had a brother called Ananda who used to visit him. There was a large patch of garden on the sides and at the back of the house. One side was a favourite cricket pitch for my brother and his friends. Gamini

Seneviratne was my brother's friend from Wesley and he continued to be our family friend until he passed away a few years ago. My mum would make a large jug of tea and lay this together with cups and saucers on a table on the front verandah so that the boys could come in and take a sip whenever they felt like it. No doubt she would also have had some biscuits or patties for them to nibble on.

We had friends across the road – the de Mottes – Charmaine, Virginia (called Virgi) Trevor and Errol – I used to run across and chat to them whenever I stood near our gate and spotted someone going into their house. This happened at least once a day! I well recall how I used to enjoy listening to music on their radio and record player – just like in our house, which was why I felt it was almost an extension of ours! I listened to the radio and sang along and even after it was switched off I would continue to sing – *I'm sending you a big bouquet of roses* – was one of my favourites. Don't ask me how the others put up with me!

I must have been about four when I began school at Wesley College Nursery which had both girls and boys attending. After the nursery level Wesley was a boys' only college. Wesley was just around the corner from where we lived so we used to just take a walk to school! I hated leaving home and going to school and wailed and whinged every single day and had to be virtually dragged to school by my mother! Once I got there however I settled down fairly well – our teachers were

Mrs Joyce Leembruggen who had the most wonderful knack of telling a story and my class teacher was young and very pretty – Miss Drieberg. My mother had asked my brother and his friends to keep an eye on me; and can you imagine a fifteen-year-old boy running down to see his baby sister who would bawl and want to be carried the minute she saw him? Looking back, I thought my mother must have been most unreasonable to expect this! Still surprisingly, my brother and his friends *did* come visit me – they even brought little sweets and toffees and spent time with me during the interval and saw me into class when the bell rang. Many many years later when I spoke to our dear family friend Gamini Seneviratne and remarked how good it was of him and my brother and others to look after me in the way they did. He gave me an amused look and then revealed that they really came to see Miss Drieberg and not me at all. After all, she certainly was a lovely young lady and they loved having some excuse to come over and take a peek at her! What delusions I had lived under all those years! His words sounded like the pop of a balloon bursting – leaving me quite deflated!

When I was about five years old I gradually began to like going to school, especially the singing and story time parts of it. I also began learning to read and write and found this to be the most exciting part of my life at that time. Soon I was competent enough to read the story of the *Ant Who Walked to Jerusalem*, and the tedious and never-ending obstacles the Ant had to face became challenges to me as well. My greatest moment was when

I learnt to spell the word Jerusalem. So thrilled I was with my achievement that whenever anyone visited our home my greeting would be, "Shall I spell Jerusalem for you?" Too taken aback to say anything in reply to this most strange form of welcome, they would say politely, "Yes of course!" Then I would immediately proceed to write the word on whatever was nearest me – the wall, a newspaper, a chair. We were also a musical family – my mother having been a music teacher and pianist and my brother played both the piano and the clarinet. My sister Lorni was also a pianist. I wanted very much to be a part of this musical group and my mother gave me a spoon and told me to keep time to the music they played – I had to tap the handle part of the spoon on a table nearby – so I felt great to be a part of the group! When I had the chance, I thumped on the piano and imagined I was a great pianist and sang at the top of my voice all the popular songs of the day. However, Lorni was the singer in the family and rendered all the popular numbers we heard over the radio with great gusto and in perfect tune. In fact, later on in my life she took it upon herself to 'teach' me how to sing properly (which I can't really do to this day!) and would sing something and help me to sing 'seconds'. It was great fun for me but would have been a pain for her and her friends – all eight years older than I was, remember – this little brat screeching all the time!

As mentioned earlier, at this time in my life, daddy worked in Matara. He stayed there during the week and came home over the weekends. We visited him sometimes and what I remember well is that we used to go by train in sleeping berths – which meant double bunks with a tiny ladder to get to the upper bed. Always a treat for me! My recollections of Matara itself are mostly the beach and the sea so I guess we must have spent a fair amount of time walking the white sands collecting shells and washing our feet in the waves as they crashed on the shore.

My father had an imagination which would enthral any child and related stories to me that I not only totally believed but which live in my memory to this day. I recall how he told me that he used to come in his own plane from Matara.

"I saw you playing in the garden today when I was coming in my plane," he would tell me. "Aha – I saw your pink dress from the skies and I waved!" He looked at me and smiled.

"You saw me from so high and you waved? Oh! Why don't you bring your plane here," I asked, hands clasped tight and eyes glistening?

He looked around at the small garden and replied, "There's no room here, I park it on Galle Face Green and then come on my horse."

"Horse? So where is the horse?" I was excited at the thought of having a horse right here with me.

"Nah – the horse had to go and have his dinner so I took a bus to get here."

So, each time I was in the garden and a plane flew overhead I made it a point to stop whatever I was doing and wave heartily, I would also shout a big hello to my father up there in the plane – just in case.

I had no idea exactly when my brother Jim fell ill. All I remember is that he began staying at home and my parents had to take him to the doctors constantly and then the doctors even began coming home to treat him. He was a brilliant pianist and clarinet player and my mother, being a music teacher, enjoyed having him play his clarinet while she played the piano. I also do recall some of his friends playing other musical instruments – the saxophone, the trumpet and even the drums. Sometimes he would just play the piano and my mum would listen and correct him as he went along. I remember these musical groups of two or three in our little sitting room having a very lively musical interlude. Then suddenly Jim stopped coming into the sitting room and remained in his own bedroom. Most of his time was spent in bed. Ultimately the piano was moved to his bedroom and from time to time he would get up and play a few tunes but the concert atmosphere had vanished.

Jim's condition must have worsened as one day my parents took the decision to move to my aunts' house at Castle Street, as he had to be hospitalised at the Central Hospital located nearby down Horton Place. This house was occupied by my father's sisters and brother (and many others as well). We had to leave our house *Smyrna* but kept someone there to look after our doggie Kim and to keep the house clean and tidy while we were at

Castle Street. I do recall visiting the house from time to time. Jim had to make several visits to the doctors and the hospital and finally he had to stay in hospital for several weeks – perhaps over a month – as he had been diagnosed with cancer in the blood – leukaemia. Leukaemia in the late nineteen forties was somewhat of a mystery disease and the doctors tried everything within their powers to pull him out of it.

The fact that Jim was critically ill was totally beyond my comprehension, after all I was just over five years old. I remember with clarity how they once gave him an 'ice bath' when his fever rose too high and how they hooked him up to machines to give him some special treatment; but all these meant absolutely nothing to me. To me, my brother was sick and in hospital and the doctors there would make him better; that's what doctors were there for weren't they? I stopped going to school now and almost every day accompanied my mum to the hospital to see my brother. I always looked forward to going to the hospital with mummy. As I said before, because of my young age I really didn't understand the severity of the situation. My association with the hospital was the large tree somewhere in the compound which shed those fire-engine red shiny *maddichchiya* seeds, and also the discarded injection phials, both of which I collected with fanatical passion. The seeds went into little square bags my mother sewed for me – something like small bean-bags, or I'd put them into containers and run my fingers through them over and over again, delighting in their smoothness. The empty phials I would use as 'milk bottles' for my dolls. I was too young to understand that these injections were being used to try to cure what was then an incurable disease. After maybe about a month they brought Jim back home from the hospital and I was overjoyed. From my point of view now we were all together again!

The Castle Street house was located diagonally opposite the famous Senanayake's house. The constitutionalists led by D. S. Senanayake succeeded by winning Independence on February 4th 1948. D. S. Senanayake became Ceylon's first Prime Minister in the same year. His son Dudley, also actively involved in politics, was the Prime Minister of the country on two occasions. I loved to watch Prime Minister D. S. ride on his horse down the road during various national celebrations. The crowd of people marching by his side and trumpets playing and drums beaten – it was a real treat for me to watch.

Number fifteen Castle Street was a rambling single floored house set in a sprawling garden, as was the style at the time. (Incidentally, at the time of writing this, it is the site for several houses belonging to my good friends Kumu and Ranjit Fernando who live there with their extended family occupying various sections of it.) Its enormous rooms, wide verandahs and corridors were filled with not only people but also dogs and cats, a mynah who whistled with single-minded persistence, and a parrot who spewed out greetings and remarks – some quite rude – to all and sundry. I recall the house being positioned somewhat in the center of the compound. There were little gardens all around – the front lawn which had some Frangipani trees and extended onto the side through a very beautiful archway bearing a perennial Allamanda creeper which went into a narrowish side garden alongside some bedrooms. The back garden was extensive – bearing large trees – mangosteen, mango, coconut, to name those I can remember. The garden on the other side was also extensive with an enormous expanse of grass with some coconut trees and a guava tree which was not too difficult to climb, and a driveway to the garage situated right at the end of it. The driveway was a popular cricket pitch and my cousins and brother – when he felt well enough – and their friends often indulged in long games during the day. The grassy lawns were perfect for having 'dolly' picnics; shrubs sprang out of unexpected corners; creepers ran over crumbling arches and there were countless trees which took turns at being laden with a variety of fruits or flowers. Occupying a corner of the large back garden was a chicken shed which held almost two dozen hens, chickens and a couple of roosters. They were confined to their coops only at night and during the day had a run of the garden, much to my delight.

Apart from myself, my parents, my brother Jim and sister Lorni, the house also had many other human occupants. There were my two aunts – my father's sisters – Phylla (Phyllida Florence) and Queenie (Hester) who were teachers at Ladies College, my uncle – dad's brother – Neville who was a pastor in the Dutch Reformed Church; then there were the much older cousins Rita and Douglas; two medical students were 'boarders' and occupied the room off the front verandah, another boarder James, lived in a room off the back verandah. There was Dinah who was adopted by my aunts and helped run the house. She soon became my best friend. Finally, there was the old *amme* who did all the cooking for the household. Various people used to come in from time to time to tidy the garden, pluck the coconuts and give the house a general cleaning. To my four/five year old mind the house and garden had no boundaries. They went on for ever and ever and there was always sufficient space for me to wander around and plenty of nooks and corners in which I could get lost in a wonderland of my own.

I wasn't sent to school any more while we were there, with my father in Matara and my mother's days fully occupied attending to the needs of my brother. At this age my world consisted of the house and garden. Then my father was transferred back to Colombo as he wanted to be with his family especially as my brother was ill and had to be constantly seeing doctors and visiting the hospital. This was the time we went to stay with my aunts at Castle Street as it was close to the medical facilities we had to deal with.

My days at Castle Street were full of adventure. I was very happy playing on my own in its vast garden filled with trees for me to climb, picking my way through a yard full of fowls and chickens and romping around with the dogs.

A world of not more than a few thousand square feet of space I reckon but for me it was a world of its own. Taking my height (two feet nothing?) into account I was closer to the ground than anywhere else. But I overcame this drawback by learning to be an adept tree climber and thereby raising my world to the level of perhaps fifteen or twenty feet off the earth, and I also enhanced the dimensions of my world through my imagination, which was nurtured by my father who delighted in telling me the most astonishing stories. My cousin Douglas fixed a swing for me – two ropes tied to a tree with a wooden plank at the bottom. This was a real adventure for me, just sitting on it and swinging into the sky and then back on earth.

My memories of this place are innumerable and clear in a jumbled kind of way (if that's possible!). My sister used to go to school on a bicycle. I could never get over how she used to just climb onto her bike and ride away all on her own. She had friends who used to do the same and often came visiting – Teruni Suhood and Pauline Mack were the names I remember! The clinkle of a bell meant it was either the postman or someone to see Lorni. I would love to run in announcing the name of the visitor in a loud voice. I must say that Lorni didn't take too well to my screaming out the names of her friends in this manner! I found it hard to imagine that this two-wheeled contraption was their chief mode of transport. Not for them the single or red double-decker buses that used to ply the roads, or the rickshaws drawn by men along the streets, or the tramcars that jingled and clanged their way on tracks along the Maradana thoroughfares. I was always amazed and quite insanely jealous at this nonchalant display of independence, for even in the present context of freedom that young girls boast of, I have still to come across this phenomenon.

Religion played an important role in our lives. My dad's family were faithful followers of the Dutch Reformed Church and my mother's side were staunch Methodists. My two aunts saw to it that Sundays were observed with the strictest Christian precepts in mind. We were not permitted to sing anything other than hymns on this special holy Day of Rest. Listening to pop songs on the radio was out of the question. I was just learning how to whistle but my accomplishment was severely crushed with a quote from the Bible. I dared not disobey the rules as I was always conscious that God's own Ambassador was living with us.

My father's brother Neville was a pastor of the Dutch Reformed Church in Colombo at the time. He was the Collegiate Minister of the Dutch Reformed Church of Ceylon (Presbyterian) and Pastor in Charge of the Churches of Galle and Matara. He was a much respected Minister in the Dutch Reformed Church at Wolvendaal as well. He was also a fully-fledged lawyer but on passing his final examination he decided immediately to be a Preacher of God's Word rather than be a Pleader of the Law. Having departed from the study of law he went to the Bangalore Theological College and later he was granted a scholarship to Princeton University (Seminary) in America from where he returned to us after graduating in Theology. He was offered the opportunity to stay on and do another degree but he chose to return to Ceylon and join the Church.

The history of the Dutch Reformed Church (now known as the Christian Reformed Church) covers 360 of the 400 years of Dutch – Sri Lankan relations. It was in Galle on the 6th of October 1642 that the first Protestant ministrations began after *Willem Jacobsz Coster* had captured the fort in 1640. The Dutch found four religions already established on the Island – Buddhism, Hinduism, Islam and Catholicism. The Portuguese had introduced the Roman Catholic religion during their rule and were determined to establish it firmly in the country.

The Dutch East India Company founded in 1602 (VOC – *Verenigde Oost-Indische Compagnie*) flourished and lasted for two centuries. It was a combination of commercial organisations in several cities of Holland and traded both in Asia and between Asia and Europe. It was also responsible for the administration of the Dutch possessions in Asia, which was mainly a trading operation and therefore did not want to make their religion take over their trade objectives. On the other hand, the Dutch did realise that with the spread of

Catholicism in the country the Portuguese could use this ploy to recapture the island. So, the Dutch administration decided that all Roman Catholic churches, monasteries, schools and any other organisations be terminated and transferred to the Dutch Reformed Church. Organised Protestantism may be said to have been introduced in 1658 after the Dutch land and sea forces had defeated the main stronghold of the Portuguese on the island, the fort of Colombo, and became the sole masters of the Maritime Provinces of Ceylon.

Uncle Neville was of medium build, fair and I remember well his round glasses which he wore all the time. I can recall his voice as being soft and gentle and his manner quiet and unassuming. One never knew when he was in and when he was out, so quietly did he enter and leave the house. At five I did know where America was – my schoolteacher aunts made it a point to show it on a map to me, when my uncle was there. It seemed so far away that it was too complicated for me to understand. With all the stories I had heard about Red Indians, White people and Black slaves, bursting through my little head, I was sure my uncle must have had a pretty rough time getting through all he had to learn in school while avoiding the arrows of the Indians. I loved the idea that they were Red! No wonder then he was so quiet and subdued in his manner.

I had, in my usual persuasive (or was it bossy?) manner, asked him whether I could 'play' in his room to which he graciously consented. I made him the guardian of my many 'bottles' of milk (a collection of injection phials filled with a mixture of flour and water 'milk' made by my mother) for my doll Kathleen. These were stored in a minute drawer located in the upper part of his desk and Kathleen used to sleep in a little cot on the floor underneath. It was at this table, which stood by the window of his room, he used to sit and write all his Sunday Sermons. I would sit at his feet giving Kathleen her milk from the minuscule 'bottle' which he had to pass down to me as and when I called for them which was about every two or three minutes. While I fed Kathleen I not only spoke to her but also sang various nursery rhymes before I lulled her to sleep. All this went on while my uncle wrote his sermons and I wouldn't have been surprised if some of the words from below had floated into his words of wisdom for the coming Sunday! Not once though, do I recall him telling me to get out of his hair (he was bald anyway) or to get the hell out of his room (he was a priest remember and didn't use the word hell carelessly).

Sadly, Uncle Neville died while we were at Castle Street. I dimly recall the day he passed away. It was afternoon (I think) when I heard my cousin Douglas give a loud shout and, in a blur, I remember people running around but the next thing I knew was that my uncle was rushed to the hospital where he died of a heart attack. It was sad that I had known him so briefly and at a time in my life when I wasn't able to really appreciate his deeper qualities.

My two unmarried aunts (dad's sisters) were teachers at CMS Ladies College and took great pride in their vocation. Two wonderful ladies they were – kind and caring but at the same time very regimented in their ideas and practices. My sister always relates the story of how when she and my brother had to stay with them for a short period to attend school while my parents were living out of Colombo, my aunts insisted they wear socks and shoes while at home. They were not allowed to wear slippers and walking barefoot was strictly taboo. So, you can imagine the hullabaloo this created. They used to wait until my aunts took their afternoon siesta and then rip off all their foot gear and run around madly! Of course, they took great care that their feet were properly shod again before my aunts woke up.

Meticulous customs and manners were observed at meal times. First the large brass gong which stood on a 'whatnot' was struck with a wooden rod giving out a deep sonorous sound. On the third or fourth beat we had to all be seated at the table ready for the meal! The sounding of the gong was the signal informing those in the house that the meal of the day had been served, and this deep sound was heard four times a day – for breakfast, lunch, tiffin, and dinner. Incidentally, a 'whatnot' – was the name given to a sturdy wooden stand consisting of three long shelves held together with very elegantly designed slim spiral supports. This was a storage area for some dishes and also a few decorative ornaments.

The dining room held the large oval shaped wooden dining table with maybe around ten to twelve chairs. My aunts insisted on a strict dress code being observed at meals eaten at the dining table; they said that this was the respect you showed for your food which was provided by the Lord above. The men wore long trousers, shirt and jacket and socks and shoes. The women wore below the knee cotton dresses and had their hair tidy – if it was long hair it was generally put back in a hairnet. I well recall how after we were all seated, my aunt would glance at my father and ask in a very polite but cold voice, "Have you forgotten something?" to which he would in an equally cold and not so polite voice say, "No." This bandying of words would go on a few times during which I wondered what it was my father kept forgetting when he came to the table. It was only much later that I learned that it was his jacket that he did not forget, but simply refused to wear to table. My father being the youngest in his family of ten (or twelve?) was I suppose a rebel in his own kind of way and refused to comply with what he considered were totally ridiculous rules his older siblings tried to impose upon him. My mother felt quite unhappy about this and used to admonish him later, and he, in his characteristic way used would guffaw, "Oh rubbish!" and dismiss the topic. This preamble was repeated so often that it became almost a routine introduction to a meal. After this little toss of words there would be a moment of silence and then my Uncle (the priest) would begin saying the Grace and we'd join in before we served ourselves our meal.

The table was always flawlessly laid, with place mats and napkins and of course the all-important cutlery. Only porcelain crockery was used at the time and a wide array of plates and serving dishes were used at the table. Serving dishes were passed hand to hand as each person served a portion onto his /her plate. Jugs of water stood at appropriate points on the table with round covers made of net edged with crocheted lace and beads. Using the fingers for eating was totally forbidden and if you so wished to indulge in this practice you had to sit at a round table specially set out on the back verandah for this purpose! I often took my place there, with cousin Douglas who sat there every day, as he not only ate with his fingers but also consumed great quantities of fried dried red chillis – the strong pungent odour from these, made all around him sneeze and teary eyed. I can't ever recall seeing him seated at the main dining table. Douglas was my 'fun' cousin. He always had some crazy idea up his sleeve and entertained me no end!

I well remember having baths on the back verandah. There was an enormous basin filled with water and I would step into it and someone would pour water over my body and soap me and then I would step out while the water was quickly replaced with clean water from some buckets standing by. I would then step inside the basin again and the soap would be washed off with the clean water. For some strange reason or another, unknown to this day, I didn't like the idea of the soapy water being thrown away and would howl my lungs out. I wanted the soap to just disappear and for the water to be clean again – like magic. My mother whose patience was by now totally worn out would admonish me in harsh tones making me howl even louder and amidst all this hullabaloo cousin Douglas would appear out of God knows where and tell me not to cry and say he would bring back all the water for me. My wonderman! He would tell me to close my eyes if I wanted this to happen and warned me that if I opened them even the slightest teeniest bit the magic would not work. I would shut my eyes so tight that they hurt and after he uttered a series of magical words in a loud and sombre voice, *Barra bara ul um bara cadabra*. I would open my eyes and lo! – there would be the basin full of water again! All very clear with no soapy suds in it.

On holidays my aunts used to take me along with them when they visited friends. My treat was travelling in a tramcar on the Maradana main road. A tramcar was a passenger vehicle the size of a bus which ran on a rail-track and powered by overhead cables. These were only to be found on certain public roads. I liked it so much that many a time they used to take me back to the main stop and then again to wherever we were headed. Such indulgence! Jumping on the tramcar and having it glide along the tracks jingling and tooting its horn as it moved was a great adventure for me. Each night before we went to bed my aunts had this great game of "Puss puss in the corner" – we stood at three corners of the large square front verandah and at a certain point we had to cross over – the one who didn't find a corner was out. Of course, they always allowed me to be the winner!

One of my greatest treats was to be taken to the Dehiwala Zoo. The Superintendent of the Zoo at that time was the legendary Aubrey Weinman – the zoo was reputed to be one of the best in this region. My aunts knew Aubrey very well – I used to call him Uncle Aubrey and I shall never forget the times when he used to go up to the cages which housed the Royal Bengal Tigers and call them to the edge of their cage and put his hand inside and pet them on their heads. The tigers would just close their eyes and then open them and look directly at him. He would speak to them while doing this and the crowd gathered around to watch this incredible scene would be absolutely silent – not a sound except the voice of Uncle Aubrey and the tiger's gruff 'purr' could be heard! I recall when my parents took me to the zoo and we watched this whole sequence again. I asked Uncle Aubrey whether I could get a job at the zoo – I loved the animals so much!

My aunt Queenie was an ardent dog lover and bred some Golden Retrievers and English Sheepdogs which she used to show in the Dog Show Competitions in Colombo. I used to go with her for the dog shows and even the training part of it enthralled me. She would walk them round in a circle, then say 'sit' in that certain tone, 'heel' in the same sort of tone and they were absolutely obedient. No wonder then that they were regular prize winners at the competitions held two or three times a year in Colombo. She used to brush them and clean them and even inspect their teeth – just like they did in the real dog show. I remember a big white fluffy English Sheepdog called Fluffy and then his son named Tony, and the most wonderful Golden Retriever called Lassie. Lassie was my favourite and I used to follow her around and have long meaningful conversations with her. I longed to have some baby Lassies to play with and plagued my parents and my aunts about this. Like all children I believed implicitly in a literal sense what any adult told me – words spouted by an older person were absolutely the Gospel Truth. To appease my constant wailings about wanting a little doggie for myself, my dad took me to the garden and picked up a *kurumbatta* (a young tiny coconut – these were golden ones from the golden thambili tree) and told me that these were Lassie's eggs, and if I collected some and made her sit on them, I could have baby Lassies in no time at all. So, I diligently searched and collected all the 'golden' *kurumbattas* I had gathered from under the coconut trees and placed them on the grass and dragged Lassie to this spot and forced her to sit on them. I had to hold her down for a few minutes and when I thought she had settled down I flopped under a nearby tree to keep an eye on her. I would then unwittingly of course, doze off to sleep and used to be in a rage when I awoke and found Lassie missing and the 'eggs' strewn all over the ground. This happened time and again with the same reactions on my part. Oh, to be a child again!

The fowls and their antics were another thing altogether. Hens roamed about with their baby chicks. I well recall a rooster of enormous proportions who displayed a feathered coat of brilliant hues. He dominated the entire lot of them and one day when I was inside talking to the kukubaas, as I fondly called the hens, the rooster perhaps thinking that I was trying to compete with him in his play with the ladies, became positively jealous and he came straight at me, wings outstretched and beak open and landed right on my head. I decided to make a run for it, to escape his fury and in doing so tripped and fell in a heap on the gravel. The feathered beast stood over me, eyes glaring into mine, beak hovering like a sickle near my face, and the next thing was that he dug his razor-edged beak into my face and continued to peck me furiously, cackling and spreading his wings in great defiance, while I struggled and screamed and literally brought the entire household running into the garden to see what the commotion was all about. My cousin Douglas, as always, came to my rescue immediately. He hounded the bird away, picked me up and took me inside. After that my mother took over (as far as I recall) and I guess she must have poured the usual solution of hydrogen peroxide to clean the wound, which was now bleeding rather profusely. The sting I felt when this was used on the wound was as bad as the attack by the rooster and set me off screeching again! I had a real nasty cut on the side of my mouth and my father was furious that this had happened and threatened my aunts who were also quite upset about the whole thing, that he would have the, "Monster killed and cooked for lunch on Sunday". Of course, although this had happened to me, I dearly loved the rooster and the very thought of him being killed was the last thing I wanted – so that began my next bout of screeching for the day!

Amidst all the fun and excitement going on in my own little world little did I realise that my brother had reached the final stages of his fatal illness. There was a constant visiting of doctors and drips and injections that were administered to him – but all this made hardly any impact on me.

Finally, the day came when my darling brother could not hold on any longer. The day on which he died is stuck in my mind – somewhat blurred but still very much there. It was a few days after my sixth birthday that this happened – on the 6th of July 1950. My dim recollections are that he passed away in the morning. My sister tells me that she and my two aunts were standing at the gate having a chat when my mother suddenly came out running and told my sister, "He's gone." She knew this meant my brother had died and couldn't help but burst into tears as she ran back into the house.

My immediate reaction, as I recall, was being totally puzzled as I could not understand what death actually meant. My parents told me that Jim had gone to stay with Jesus – they felt this was some kind of comforting message for me. The funeral and gathering of friends and relations who came to the house was a time of rushing around for me and it did not occur to me that I would never see my brother again; in my child's mind I was convinced that he would suddenly appear at the door one day. Today I look upon this as one of the saddest moments of my life. Not only because he left us but because I never really got to know him. In my mind I still see him, a tall fair boy wearing glasses, keenly bent over the piano playing the keys with great intent or with a clarinet held to his lips piping out a melodic tune. I try hard to imagine what his voice was like, but it never seems to work. Needless to say, my parents and sister would have been absolutely devastated when he died. The thought did not cross my mind that I would never have my brother by my side again.

We left Castle Street some weeks later and cleared up our house at Karlshrue Gardens. It was good to see the old house again and I loved having my doggie Kim back in my life. But I did feel the emptiness. The void of someone missing in my life, of not having a piano in the house and mostly not having a brother to play his exquisite music and have him chat to me and have his friends over for games of cricket. I cannot imagine what it must have been for my family to deal with this irreparable loss. Of course, we used to visit our aunts quite often and had many meals with them and my cousins but the absence of my brother was very much felt at these family gatherings.

And so, life went on. Then came the time when my father (who had by now passed all the necessary exams to take up a posting in the Civil Service) mentioned that there was a proposition of him being transferred out of Colombo. I didn't understand what the word 'transfer' meant and he explained that he would be sent to work in a town out of Colombo. He went on to explain that he would take all of us with him – he wouldn't be leaving us behind.

The story goes that my father was offered Polonnaruwa as the next posting, but when he visited the place to check things out, he discovered that there was no school at the time available there for us to attend and we would have to live in Colombo as we did when he worked in Matara. But this was too soon after my brother had died, and my dad was determined to keep our family together as he felt we needed one another more than ever, especially after the sad loss we had just experienced. The next offer was Trincomalee, which, when he visited, pleased him no end. The house was perfect and the Convent which we would attend was very highly recommended and was just a two-minute walk from the house. So, Trinco – as it was called – was to be our next destination.

My mother was quite busy packing our belongings together. Large cardboard boxes held all the contents of our house. This included kitchen utensils, crockery and cutlery, ornaments, our clothes and other personal items, our books and a hundred other things! Large lorries appeared at our gate and the furniture was packed in very carefully. Then in went the boxes and finally we climbed into our little car with a driver and ventured forth into our new destination. I was sad to leave Colombo and my aunts' house which had been a home to me for so many months. I was also sad to leave Karlshrue Gardens because I had made many friends in the neighbourhood but the saddest part was seeing the piano being taken away and my brother's original room being cleared. Little did I realise that I would never come back to live at Karlshrue Gardens. This time my father was taking our whole family – including our doggie Kim. Although at that time I didn't fully understand that my brother had physically left us, this new determination of my father to keep all members of our home together – even our little quadruped! – was in retrospect evidence that we were leaving forever, the home we shared until my brother's death – with its memories of a time before we met the pain of loss. Only later on did I understand that the move to Trinco was a chance for my family to pick themselves up again, especially after the tragedy of losing my brother. I cannot imagine how hard it must have been for my parents and sister to deal with this loss. The loss of a child is no doubt one of the most traumatic experiences for a family to endure, and cannot be explained in words.

Jim, my brother and me at Smyrna.

Lorni is ten years old and I am two years old, at the Castle Street house.

Mummy, Lorni and myself at my brother Jim's grave, 1950.

Mummy, Lorni and myself with the driver leaving Smyrna for the Castle Street house.

PART TWO

TRINCOMALEE
Jan 1951 – Dec 1952

Before we left, my dad took it upon himself to tell me the story of Trincomalee! We sat down on the verandah and he showed me a map of Ceylon and pointed out to where Trincomalee was located. It was on the East Coast. Then he explained – it is the anglicised (English) form of the Tamil word 'Tiru-kona-malai' meaning 'Lord of the Sacred Hill' which is a reference to the town's ancient Konneswaran Temple. It is often referred to by its shortened form 'Trinco'.

And so, the story went – a lesson in history! The Portuguese built a Fort in Trinco in 1623 which was captured by the Dutch in 1638. It was attacked and taken over by the French in 1672. They handed it back to the Dutch East India Company (VOC) when the Paris Peace Treaty was signed in 1784. In 1795 the British attacked and defeated the Dutch, and took over the Fort. The British renamed it Fort Frederick in 1803 in honour of Frederick, Duke of York. With this, Trincomalee was in the hands of the British and this became their first land acquisition in Ceylon. During World War ll the British made Trincomalee the headquarters of the Combined Allied Forces in South Asia. The Japanese carried out an air raid on Colombo on Easter Sunday April 5th 1942 and moved on towards Trinco but the British had already taken the precaution of sending a fleet to sea and only two ships were destroyed by the Japanese. So Trincomalee remained under British rule until Ceylon gained Independence in 1948.

The importance of Fort Frederick was mainly because of Trinco's natural harbour. The harbour was strategically located which suited the purposes of naval surveillance for the British during the Second World War. It was believed that a strong naval force could secure control of India's Coromandel Coast. Trincomalee had earned the title of being one of the finest deep water natural harbours in the world. These comments came from none other than Admiral Arthur Wellesley – later the Duke of Wellington – who became famous when he defeated Napoleon – while he was a Colonel in the British East India Company. Wellesley occupied a house in Fort Frederick in 1799 – named Wellington House (or Wellesley Lodge) which still exists. At the same time Midshipman Horatio Nelson (later Lord Nelson) also visited Trincomalee and he too described the harbour as one of the finest in the world. Before the Second World War the British built the Royal Air Force base at China Bay and used it as an oil and fuel storage facility.

He went on to tell me about the history behind the job he had undertaken. The Ceylon Civil Service was the main administrative body of the Ceylon Government which was under British colonial rule in the immediate post-independence era. It was commonly known by its acronym CCS and was established in 1833. The

CCS functioned as an important part of the executive administration of the country until Ceylon gained independence in 1948, but was abolished in 1963 and the Ceylon Administrative Service was formed.

My dad who was in the CCS was appointed as the Office Assistant in Trincomalee and was responsible to the Assistant Government Agent in Trinco and the Government Agent of the area (who at that time was based in Batticaloa) for the proper supervision of the numerous Government departments located within the region. These included the arrival/departures of ships to the Trincomalee harbour, observing the relevant Customs rules and regulations, and also matters involving the Police and legal administration and also Local & General Electoral procedures in the area. He also had to pay regular 'circuit' visits to the surrounding towns which came under the jurisdiction of the main Government office in Trincomalee.

We moved to Trincomalee at the end of 1950 when I was just six and a half years old. We were right in time for us to begin attending our new school, St Mary's Convent in January 1951. My mum, dad, sister Lorni – and also our beloved doggie Kim – piled into our little Austin car to travel to Trinco. We couldn't take the train as dogs were not permitted in trains – so our road trip went on for hours! In addition, my dad had an official driver – so we were totally cramped in the car with Kim sitting on our laps to add to it! We stopped once on the way to have a snack. We reached Trinco late that evening and a government official met us at a certain point and led us to our new abode.

We were greeted by the awesome sight of a lovely spacious bungalow which was of Dutch architectural design. We drove through a long driveway and parked our car under a large portico which stood in front of the house. We faced a verandah which seemed never ending! Later, I discovered that it was around eighty feet long and fifteen feet wide. It was supported on the sides by enormous rounded Dutch pillars. The verandah spanned the entire front of the house and took a little turn at one end which led to a set of two rooms on that side of the house. My father used the first room as his office room, and the one behind which had a separate entrance from the back verandah was used as a guest room – this had an attached bathroom. Our spacious bedrooms were located on the opposite side of the house. My sister had a corner bedroom, and my parents and I adjoining quarters. A large bathroom stood at the end of the bedroom area, which we all shared. The centre of the house consisted of an extensive sitting and dining room. The rear of the house consisted of a long corridor which had many enclosed rooms leading off it. These were used as the kitchens and quarters for the domestic staff. One of these rooms was later turned into a poultry shelter for the roosters and hens we acquired. My mother being an excellent cook, converted the first room into her kitchen so that she could go in there and make whatever she wanted! The main kitchen was in the next area.

The house was referred to as the OA's Bungalow – immediately next to it on one side stood the Trincomalee Resthouse. On the other side of the bungalow (divided by a roadway) was a large mansion called Admiralty House where the head of the Navy based at Trinco lived and where in earlier times was occupied by Admiral Sir Charles Austen (younger brother of author Jane Austen.) He died in Trincomalee and his grave can be found in the cemetery in Trinco. This grand two-storeyed mansion was wonderfully decorated with large doors and windows and chandeliers suspended from the ceilings. The weekends were generally busy with parties being held and I used to love to stand at our gate or sit atop our low boundary wall gazing at the guests all grandly clad walking in and out, and what held me spellbound were the glittering lights from the chandeliers. Sadly, this mansion was destroyed during the recent civil war in Sri Lanka. After the war it was reconstructed and has been turned into a museum.

Something that fascinated me was that in our dining room and sitting room there were *punkahs* which stood over us. The word *punkah* is of Hindi origin deriving from the word *pankh* which meant the wings of a bird which produced a slight draft when flapped. In the British colonial age, the word was used to describe a swinging fan made from a local type of palm leaf which was fixed on a rattan frame and fastened to the ceiling. The 'Punkah Wallah' or the 'Punkah Coolie' was the name given to the man who worked the 'punkah'. He sat on the floor below the 'punkahs' and drew the strings which hung down. As he pulled them to and fro the punkah swung back and forth (like a swing) and sent out a lovely cool breeze to those seated below. My father would like to relax in the evenings when he came back after work and we would all sit around in the sitting room and chat – and the punkah man would appear and sit cross legged on the floor and start pulling the strings which made the punkahs swing back and forward sending down a wonderful breeze! I would absolutely love to watch this whole exercise – in fact I recall also trying pull on the strings myself – to the horror of the punkah puller! Then at the dinner table the same routine would continue. Sometimes the punkah would make a kind of squeaky sound as it swayed up and down! The noise of the punkah made my dad very irritated as it interfered with our evening chats! He would ask us about school and my mum would speak about friends and all the happenings during the day but this was all completely drowned with the punkah noise! So, within a few weeks my dad tactfully 'retired' the punkah man and got some ceiling fans installed which gave us all the cool breeze we needed! But the punkahs were kept on just as a symbol of past times – and they did fascinate our visitors, many of whom had never seen these before! The punkah man took up to helping the garden cleaners!

What was very noticeable was the extremely rigid caste system in Trincomalee. For instance, we had many workers in our garden and house. Maybe about three for the garden and another two to clean up the house daily. The cook and a permanent cleaner lived within the premises. They belonged to different castes and would not cross one another's path even during their work. There was a separate small gate on the side of the back garden where those belonging to the 'lower' caste had to enter. The ones who belonged to a 'higher' caste came through a small gate located in front. But none of them were permitted to enter or exit through the large front gate. They had to bathe at separate wells – those who cleaned the house and the cook could bathe at a well closer to the house because they were of a higher caste, the others at a well located far into the back garden. Anyway – my father being my father ☺ said this was all nonsense and he would not tolerate this kind of behaviour in HIS house – remember he was in charge now! So, he locked the back gate and the small front gate and told all of them to enter and leave through the large front gate. And also, that they could bathe at the large well near the house. Needless to say, they took some time to get used to this very unusual attitude and to adapt to this new routine.

In front of the house lay an enormous esplanade – called the 'maidan' (this word derives from an Indian word meaning park or recreational grounds) – beyond which lay the sea. The entrance driveway to the house was quite long and surrounded by a large front garden. A low brick wall stood at the edge of the garden bordering the roadway. During the day I would often sit on this wall with my dog Kim and watch the sea and the waves and the birds flying up in the sky! The crashing of waves could be heard right up to our gate. We would also watch the people and the few vehicles which included buggy carts and bullock carts which passed by on the road. During certain seasons of the year a strong wind called the *kachan* blustered through that region and it was considered very unsafe to be out in the open at this time.

The garden was enormous. Lawns covered the front area and the two sides of the house. Huge trees stood at the edges. Flowering plants grew on the front lawn. The back garden was quite extensive and ended in several sets of stables, as occupants in the years gone by had bred horses. There was a well situated on one side of the garden, securely covered with a pulley and a bucket for the workers to have their baths. At the farthest end stood an enormous tamarind tree, which fascinated me as I could never see the top of it – it was so high. My sister who was nearly fourteen, was an expert tree climber, and would race up the tree making me feel quite helpless and envious. I recall how once, on a dare, she climbed very high up on a tamarind tree, and couldn't come down! What a calamity! Ultimately my father had to call the fire brigade to bring their ladders and get her down!

Trincomalee was a small, not too crowded town at that time. My father's office, the Kachcheri, was a short drive away from our bungalow. He would generally drive himself to the office but at the same time had an 'official' driver if he ever had to go out of town on work.

The word Kachcheri is a Hindustani word first used for the Revenue Collector's Office in the early years of the British Colonial Administration in Ceylon. Revenue collection was a main feature of the Dutch pattern of colonial administration. In the first half of the nineteenth century, the British colonial administrators moved towards a more systematic form of government with civil and revenue administration. Thus, the collector's office, which continued to be locally known as the kachcheri was converted into the Government Agent's Office.

Trincomalee remained as a British naval base until 1957. The Dockyard was the Naval base in Trinco and most of the occupants at the time we were there were British. Anyone living outside this area had to have a special pass to enter its premises. We had friends within the Dockyard and used to visit them often – my father had an official pass of course, and we – as his family – were permitted to accompany him. We were delighted to meet the brother of our friend James, who stayed at my aunts' place at Castle Street, at the Dockyard. His name was Alan Thompson. He was an Anglo Indian (half North Indian and half British) and worked in the Dockyard. Alan's hobby was carpentry and as we grew to be close friends, he used to love to make all kinds of things for us! He made us an ironing board and some racks and cupboards. To this day we have the ironing board which he made and only recently did we have to renew the folding legs – after almost 65 years! That's how good the wood was at that time! He also made us a radiogram – a wooden chest which held a radio and a record player in one unit. He finally left Trinco after some years to work in one of the other British colonies. We used to keep in touch with him for some time but later on heard that he had gone back to England. He had a friend called Stanley de Silva who shared his love for carpentry and they would both come to our place to create all these wonderful things for us!

In our vast rear garden, we had our own poultry run with a number of hens and roosters and I used to delight in collecting the eggs from the straw padding on which the hens laid them. Like at my Castle Street home I used to spend much time with my 'kukoobaas' and wander along with them as they roamed the gardens. Amazingly at a certain time each evening, just as darkness was setting in, they always returned to their little home run in the backyard which was amply secured against any wild animals attacking them. I would sit with them but my memory was still rather fresh with the rooster attack at my aunts' place and I would hesitate to be over friendly with the roosters here! One morning as I was playing out in the garden, I was stunned to see a young cockerel from our yard running wildly all over with blood spurting out of his neck. To add to the horror, he was headless! I screamed and ran inside. When I was told that the old man running behind this hapless creature was the man who killed the chickens for us to eat, I was absolutely shocked. In my mind, my parents took on the role of demons and I threw the best tantrum ever I'm sure, rolling on the ground, beating my head and ramming my fists into the floor. How could they do this? Kill our chickens for us to EAT! What sort of treatment was this? What other horrors were taking place in our backyard? After much consoling my parents promised never to do this again. To my memory they never did. The rest of the poultry were cared for in the most loving manner, even being transported to Kurunegala in a separate lorry when we were transferred after two years.

Although Trinco was a wonderful experience for me I would often sit and think of my brother. Was I ever going to see him again? Would we go down to Colombo to bring him here? These are questions I asked my parents and wondered why they looked sad and told me he was with Jesus now. So, wasn't Jesus here with us now – then where was my brother? The fact that I would not see him here with me didn't quite register in my child's mind. Every time we visited Colombo, I thought we were going to bring him back with us.

I loved to run around our large garden with my English Sheepdog Kim. I used to sit on the low boundary wall in front of our house hugging Kim, and gaze at the maidan facing our place, and the waves of the sea splashing just beyond that. Kim used to follow me all over! Once he even came to my school, which scared everyone as they thought this large fluffy dog was a 'white lion'! Quite crazy! But he was running around our class and when he saw me came right up to me – so I immediately ran out of the class and of course he followed me as he usually did – and I dashed straight home! Once there my mum instructed the gardener and all household staff to always keep the front gate locked!

Lorni and I attended St Mary's Convent, which was a stone's throw away from our house. The Carmelite Sisters in charge taught us not only to read and write but also to sing, dance and sew and soon I became a part of their tradition, learning Catechism so well I could recite the Hail Mary and Holy Mary within a blink! I would pay regular visits to the grotto where a statue of Mary – Mother of Jesus – was enshrined which was located in the school compound. I would also spend time cleaning up the surroundings and keeping the front garden of the convent neat and tidy – a task put to us students on certain days of the week. I would even go on a Saturday morning to do my turn in cleaning up for the school! My mother realised that my short skirts were not an appropriate dress to wear to the convent and she immediately made me some new ones all below my knees! She loved to sew and used to make all our clothes – not an uncommon practice at that time.

During our time in Trinco, I recall names of people we knew, such as the de Kauwes – aunty and uncle and the children were Roma, Dagmar (who was in my class), Roderick and Malcolm. We used to visit them and sing songs together and wasn't it such fun! The Arentsz family – Aunty was a professional seamstress. Barbara, Yolande, Beulah, Olga, Therese –called Tootsie and who was in my class – Joy, Anton and Desmond.

The Claessans – Girla was with Lorni, the Candappas – I remember Cynthia and her sister Marie who was my classmate, the Henricus family, the Roosemale-cocq brothers Alistair and Trevor; I also recall the names Thelma Enas and Oscar Fox and the sisters Joyce and Doris Plunkett. The Assistant Government Agent at the time was Mr Tilak Gunaratna. He and his family occupied a splendid house which was built on a cliff high that overlooked the ocean. Their daughter Janaki and I were friends and we used to visit them often. My special treat was to gaze at the sea from the heights of the garden which surrounded their house. Then there was the Reimers family – Glen and Robin were close friends and they would come over often to spend the day and we used to have a great time running around the garden and climbing trees. Once I well recall we threw some stones at a beehive and were stung almost to death when a whole swarm of infuriated bees descended upon us! We ran for our life's worth screaming and yelling our lungs out – and I am certain were stung a couple of times and my mother had to shut the doors of the house to prevent the bees from coming inside. Of course, the gardeners and other workers knew exactly what to do and whatever they did, the bees left us within half an hour or so and we were able to come out again. Once outside we felt safe and secure – then we were thundered upon by my mother who warned us very severely *never never never* disturb a beehive ever again. I think she threatened to lock us up if we disobeyed her. We didn't know which was worse – chasing the bees or my mother ticking us off!

During our first few weeks my parents tried to make themselves familiar with the social circle they would encounter over the next two years. The Methodist Church was one of the first places they contacted and the pastor and other senior members of the Church were only too happy to have some new members in their congregation. They gave my parents a list of those registered as members of the Church so that they could have an idea of those who were in the congregation. I well recall my mother going through this list with a puzzled look on her face and on being asked why, by my father, she replied that there seemed to be very few Ceylonese on the list – most of them were English names like Jones, John, Smith and Milton – there was even a Shakespeare! Of course, when we did go to the Sunday service we discovered that these very English names belonged to Tamil devotees who had been converted to Christianity. Many of the converts requested that they take on the names of the foreigners who had sponsored their education and livelihood costs so that they could be remembered in the future generations of their families.

The Salvation Army played an important role in Trinco. They were located down a lane in the middle of the town. It was a large expanse of land and a spacious single storeyed building which included a hostel for children and visitors and rooms for meetings of the members and other activities. I well remember how we

Boy who worked for us, and our doggie Kim, Trinco, 1951 to 1952.

Lorni and myself in Trinco with the resthouse next door.

Me on the tricycle gifted by my parents, Trincomalee.

Mummy, Lorni with her cat, Mummy's sister Aunty Thelma and her two children Lausanne and Ian, and me with cat and our lovely English Sheepdog Kim seated by us, 1952.

Myself as a flower girl for a wedding, 1951.

My dad and his Austin car, Trincomalee.

My cousins Lausanne & Ian with sister Lorni in the centre and me in front! Trinco – that's the front gate!

Seated on the front lawn in Trincomalee with my mum, her sister Aunt Thelma, my sister Lornie, cousin Lausanne, cousin Ian and myself with Kim our dog.

My dog Kim and me on our wall at Trinco.

Verandah of our home in Trinco 1951-52.

used to go there for our Sunday School morning service and used to sing some lovely choruses and hymns. We were asked to select a chorus and I would always choose *In the Army of the King we're Marching* because I knew that then we would carry the Salvation Army flag and walk out from one gate and march down the road while singing and then get back through the next gate! My sister used to sternly warn me not to keep on selecting this as the sun was scorching at that time of day and we had to walk through the traffic on the road which was quite narrow and it was far too long a process! We also became close friends of Captain Berry and Mrs Berry and their son Peter and daughter Valerie and also Captain Freda Lamb. For Captain Lamb it was a long walk from the Salvation Army to her living quarters and she would often stop over at our place to take a break from the scorching sun! It was never a surprise to come out from our bedrooms after our afternoon siesta to find Captain Lamb asleep on the couch in our sitting room! I loved going to their Sunday School and thoroughly enjoyed singing all their lively choruses.

I made several good friends in school and they would often come over to our place on a Saturday to spend the day. We had great fun climbing the trees and playing hopscotch – there were two different types of hopscotch – one was called *aeroplane* hopscotch where there were three single squares then a double, a single and a double again – the shape resembling that of an aeroplane hence its name. The other was four double squares where one had to push a 'batta' from square-to-square hopping on one leg all the time until the final shove out of the last square. This was the more difficult one as one had to keep a steady balance all through the game unlike the other one where there were rests in between in the double squares. The batta was the winning point – the smoother it was the easier to push on to the next square. Each one had a different choice – some went for smooth stones but I always chose the large black seed of the flamboyant flower as we had several trees in the garden. The other popular game was marbles in which I had become quite an expert. After our games we would gather round the tea table on the back verandah and wallop a yummy tiffin of mummy's cakes and patties which she turned out for us.

We had a regular turnover of visitors. Relatives and friends were intrigued with the whole concept that Trinco was so far away from Colombo and would often come over to spend a couple of weeks with us, exploring the nearby attractions or just walking along the beach. My mother would be busy as usual turning out patties and cakes for tiffin and delicious lunches and dinners. I don't know what the cook actually did – maybe he cooked for the staff we had and washed the dishes! We seemed to have a stack of bikes in the house so it was no problem to do our rounds through the town and its outskirts. I was of course too young to do this but always had someone who would take me on the bike!

Looking back, I cannot get over how we – myself at just over six, my sister almost fifteen and maybe one or two friends or cousins from Colombo aged under 20 or thereabouts, used to go cycling to Periyakulam tank which was several miles from where we lived, but we thought nothing of just getting on our bikes (remember I just sat smug on the bar while the cyclist had to do all the hard work!) and riding into the sunset. I recall my cousin Allister Bartholomeusz and our good family friend Gamini Seneviratne visiting us very often. The first thing they did was take the bikes for a trip out. They would grab them and my sister being an excellent cyclist would get on her bike and set off. As always, I just sat on the bar (generally on Gamini's bike), with a cap pressed firmly on my head as I couldn't stand the sun, and enjoyed the ride! We had no mobile phones, no IDs – no emergency fallback at all if something were to happen on the way. But we didn't bother a jot; we just went – chatting and laughing all the way. On the way we would spot the large divul (woodapple) trees that lined certain parts of the road. Gamini and Allister would immediately stop and climb these trees to collect some fruit. We would take these back home with us. The ripe ones we ate either plain or with sugar and the green ones we turned into a delicious sambol with chilli powder, salt and lime. We would browse around the tank ambling along savouring nature at its fullest. After a short break we would once again climb upon our bikes and head out back home.

I well recall our friend Bertram Rulach – a surveyor by profession and also a wildlife enthusiast – arriving at our place with large writhing gunny bags which he placed on our verandah floor and opened to release a flood of snakes – much to our absolute horror. The snakes (don't ask me what kind they were!) would slither all over the place and Bertram and his assistant would dash behind them catching them expertly by their necks and putting them according to their species into separate sacks. After one of these episodes with the chaos that ensued – all of us running inside screaming, the dog going completely berserk and being dragged in and locked up, snakes skidding around at great speed (surprise to us) into all sorts of nooks and corners and Bertram and the boy shouting and running behind them – after the commotion and amazingly the fact that all the snakes were now safely ensconced in their own containers, my mother took a very firm stand with Bertram and told him he could visit us but NO SNAKES INSIDE THE HOUSE! He did visit us fairly often – but all the sorting out was done in our large backyard while we stayed locked inside the house! Bertram used to supply the zoo with different types of snakes for their collection.

Ceylon being within the Commonwealth, was under strong British influence at that time. The King of England was George VI, and we looked to the monarchy with great respect and awe. His elder daughter Princess Elizabeth was to visit Trinco while we were stationed there. I was thrilled to be one of the many little flower presenters to the Princess when she was due to visit the town and us five girls who were assigned to this task were taught the delicate art of curtsying while presenting the bouquet of flowers to the Princess. I was not only thrilled to be chosen to do this but also took my work very seriously and every second of my life I spent practising curtsying the correct way! Unfortunately, the King died at this time and Princess Elizabeth – who was the successor to the throne – was called back immediately to England while on her African tour (she was due to visit Ceylon soon afterwards) to be crowned Queen Elizabeth II in 1952. Needless to say, I was heartbroken that I wasn't going to meet the Princess and show off my perfect curtsey! My only consolation was that I was allowed to watch the film of her coronation as many times as I wished. I must have seen it at least three or four times. However, she did visit as Queen in 1954 when I lived in Kurunegala, but my only glimpse of her was that we all gathered at the railway station and waved as she sat in a train which was taking the Royal party from some place back to Colombo, I believe. The train did slow down almost to a complete halt and she smiled and waved a very royal wave and I smiled and waved wildly in return. Whether she noticed this little mite behaving in this most un-royal manner is something I will never really know but at the time I swore that she looked straight at ME and waved. So there!

As for entertainment, I can never forget the Carnival that was held once a year on the maidan. Apart from the usual stalls filled with eats and toys and crackers, there was something called the 'Well of Death' and this is what will always stick in my memory. There was this deep well made out of concrete and maybe about twenty feet deep. The spectators would be seated right around this well and a guy on a motorcycle would come out from the side and stop and wave and greet the audience. We would all clap and shout and the next thing we knew was that he would get on to the edge of the well and zoom around the sides at a tremendous speed – he would do this many times over with all those around him screaming and shouting and clapping – a deafening sound of the bike roaring along, the people shouting and loud music playing at the same time. He would go to the bottom of the well and then come up again. Finally, when he came out into the open in front of where we sat, he was greeted with a rave of shouts and applause. Sometimes there were two guys who did this together – it was the scariest thing to watch because you always felt they would crash into each other – but they never did – not when we saw them anyway!

The other bit of entertainment was the 'Fire divers' – we would go high up a rocky hill and sit around on chairs or sometimes on the ground and watch this spectacular event. A short distance from where we sat was a cliff that overlooked the sea – maybe about 100 feet high. A man would walk to the edge, and someone would set his clothes on fire and then we saw this burning image dive into the depths of the waters below. There would have been about three others who would follow this same routine and it was simply amazing to see this moving fire shoot into the waters. These are two feats that I have never seen since and they will always stick in my brain!

Every month on a small part of the esplanade there were cock-fighting events. I loved hens and cockbirds and wanted very much to see them. I thought it was just a playing game and little did I realise how terrible it was! When we sat in the group watching this we saw two lovely roosters enter the grassy patch. Then the two men in charge of them stood behind and pushed them to and fro until the birds began to peck and claw each other. The onlookers had placed bets on the winner and kept cheering as the fight went on. The shouting from the onlookers grew louder and the birds were screaming as blood poured down their feathers and one even had his eye completely pecked out! Then he fell down – dead. The onlookers cheered, whistled and clapped their hands. I started screaming and crying and my parents picked me up and whisked me back home. They couldn't believe what they had seen and also understood my total trauma at this most gruesome sight. This was something I hated and even now the mere thought of it makes me want to scream.

As a family we often visited other surrounding areas as well. When cousins and friends visited from Colombo we took them all over the town and also to the outer areas. We had many friends – mostly Government Servants – who resided within Fort Frederick and we often walked over to visit them and loved to roam among the herds of spotted deer that lived there. As mentioned earlier, the Fort was originally built by the Portuguese and during the Dutch invasion the Fort was destroyed. The Dutch then rebuilt the Fort and this is what stands today. We also loved going up Swami Rock and gazing down at the churning waves hundreds of feet below. On Swami Rock, a promontory cliff at the edge of the Fort, stood the famous Koneswaram Kovil dedicated to the Hindu God Shiva, and by the side was Lover's Leap from where according to the legend, a Dutch maiden is believed to have cast herself from the cliff as she watched her faithless lover, a seaman, sail away. I would gaze down from this great height and imagine what it must have been like to jump off this cliff in a moment of desperate sadness. When friends visited, as they often did, we also went exploring around the rocks by the beach opposite our house. No rock was too steep or too rough or too smooth for us to climb. We just climbed! We went fishing and spent hours ending our famous catch with some hideous looking black fish whose identity totally escapes me.

At that time, Rodney Jonklaas was the Assistant Superintendent of the Colombo Zoo in the days when the Dehiwala Zoo was one of the best in the world, He was an authority on marine life and had discovered some unusual species of fish in these waters. He had also invited Arthur C Clarke to explore the wrecks off the coast of Ceylon and film the magic of the sea and glorious reefs of this magic Isle. Arthur C. Clarke and photographer Mike Wilson had visited Trincomalee where they discovered the temple's underwater city and ruins. This has been described in Clarke's book *Reefs of Taprobane.*

The hot water wells at Kinniya were a popular place for us to visit. I recall that there were about twelve wells and they had different temperatures – some were at boiling point and some just warm. Lots of people would gather here to bathe in the belief that the waters had some therapeutic powers over their bodies. We sometimes drove to the Kantalai tank and had a picnic besides its waters, or to Muttur where stood the 'White Man's Tree' which is a large tamarind tree which was the place where Robert Knox is said to have been captured by the King of Kandy, Rajasinghe II. Robert Knox was detained in Ceylon from the age of 19 to 38, after the ship which his father captained for the East India Company was forced to pull in here, and they were captured. This was in 1660. Knox was held captive until he escaped in 1679. When we visited Muttur we got across the waters on a ferry. On a recent visit to Trinco, I discovered that all the earlier ferries have been removed and motorable bridges built across the spans of water one has to pass to get to many of the places in that area. The ferries no doubt took a longer time to get over, but we did have great fun going on them.

We used to visit Pigeon Island which is located close to Nilaveli. This is where the blue Rock pigeons used to breed and the surrounding waters are filled with multi coloured fishes and is ideal for snorkelling enthusiasts! Today it is a very popular visiting point for tourists. Another favourite place to visit was China Bay where Marble Beach is located. The surrounding blue waters are crystal clear and relatively calm so bathing was safe here. Also, it is called Marble Bay because of the marble stones which are found in that area. Welcombe Hotel located on Orr's Hill was another place we used to visit. Of course, in the 1950s it was a small homely place and not the luxurious hotel it has been turned into to make it a favourite tourist resort. So, visitors were always entertained to the ultimate with all these fantastic places to see and experience.

My other delight was to accompany my dad on his trips into the harbour when he had to visit the ships that were docked there. This was a part of his official duties as Office Assistant. He would travel in a small launch and I'd sit on the long side seats with my hand flicking the spray from the churning waves as we zoomed along. Once we reached the ship, we had to climb a narrow very steep gangway to get on board and then my dad would do his work while I just mooched around peering over the deck and looking at the sea. Then we would make our journey back and it was always fun to try and spot the landing jetty which would mean that we were nearing home.

We looked forward to accompanying my father on his trips to Colombo where he had to report to the Head Office. It was good to catch up with our relatives and friends there. We would stay at my aunt's place then. We always left early in the morning and reached Colombo in so many hours having stopped over at some resthouse on the way for lunch. But the return trip was different. We would leave Colombo at about 6 in the evening in our small Austin car. When we got to Habarana it would be quite late at night – chugging along in that old Austin. Then he would stop the car and we would hear thrashing sounds in the jungle surrounding us.

"Shh – stay very quiet otherwise you won't be able to see them," my dad would whisper and we would stay mouse still and silent.

The elephants would come out of the jungle and cross the road over to the other side. A whole herd of them. Fathers, mothers, singles, babies moving carefully in the protective shadow of their mothers, would saunter over, trumpeting in spurts and grunting and making a shuffling noise with their gigantic bodies. We would wait in the darkness, car lights dipped low, not a sound from us, just peering hard into the moonlit shadows, trying to see what was happening in there. Then the elephants would disappear into the thick forest and soon the sounds couldn't be heard. We waited perhaps another five or ten minutes just to be sure they had gone and then started our journey again.

One day in quite a casual conversation my parents were having with friends at a party they related this experience and those who heard this were shocked beyond words.

"Are you MAD?" they exclaimed. "You should leave Colombo early morning so you can get here before it gets dark – otherwise the wild elephants at Habarana will get you – you have to avoid that."

My father being my father – never believed that animals could do anyone any harm as much as people could (not far wrong in a kind of way I guess!) was quite taken aback and would have argued against this line of thought but with one sharp glance he got from my mother he was compelled to fall in line, and thereafter we never travelled at night!

Our years in Trinco were memorable ones for me. It was a different place and we made many dear friends, saw a totally different side of our country and experienced a different lifestyle. My saddest memory however was that our dog Kim had to be put down while we were there. There was a very virulent spread of rabies at the time and many people who had contracted the disease were hospitalised and died a hideous death. Kim unfortunately had been bitten by a rabid dog and was suspected of being a carrier of this dreadful disease. To this day I cannot help but feel a profound sense of sadness when I think of how we had to put him down. We didn't have a dog for some time after this tragic incident, and it was only when we went to Kurunegala that we got ourselves one.

In January 1953 my father was transferred again. This time it was to Kurunegala – the capital of the North Central Province. I was very sad to leave Trinco and felt I had just made it my home again and it was too soon to change. But there it was. Soon our house was turned into a rumble of packing our belongings into boxes. Moving itself was a huge job. My father had gone some weeks before and made arrangements to tidy up the house at Kurunegala and have it ready for our arrival.

The last week before we left, I spent most of my time sitting on the low wall in front of our house looking out at the maidan and the sea – thinking of the many times when Kim and I used to sit on this wall. I sat gazing at the resthouse and the convent walls, and at Admiralty House. Then walking to the back garden, peering into the well and gazing up at the gigantic tamarind tree I loved so much.

The day we left Trinco is something I will always remember. For the umpteenth time I walked around the house and its emptiness created a deep void within me. The garden was still there, with its large trees and lawns, and the well where I used to enjoy bathing sometimes, gazed back at me as I peeped over its edge. Then, my final look at the front wall where I used to sit with my beloved Kim, brought tears to my eyes. Outside the gate I gazed at the maidan and remembered how the grounds in front of the convent was where we, as students, used it as a sports exercise area. And the beautiful sea of course still crashing on the rocks nearby – sending me messages of farewell. We climbed into our car and followed the lorry with our darling ageing hens and their chickens and started off on our journey.

I knew that in Kurunegala there would be no sea and I had to once again face a whole new place, new faces, new school. My parents assured me of a good time ahead and although it was sad to leave, I knew I had to be brave and face the future with optimism.

As we passed my old school, I took my last look at it, remembering the wonderful times I spent there over the past years. I sat still and quiet in my seat, my mother put her arm around me and held me close. My sister sat on the other side and looked out of the window and my dad sat in front next to the driver. I hugged the pillow by my side and imagined it was my darling doggie Kim – tears ran down my cheeks. Would my brother come to Kurunegala? By this time in my life, I had a strange feeling that he wouldn't come back to us and my heart sank when I sensed I would never see him again.

The driver turned on the engine and silence embraced us as we moved on to our new destination – Kurunegala.

PART THREE

KURUNEGALA
Jan 1953 – Dec 1954

I was eight plus when we had to go to Kurunegala and we stayed there until I was ten plus – when my dad was transferred to Colombo. By now I knew I would never see my brother again and really missed having him with us.

It took quite a few hours to reach Kurunegala. Once again, my parents explained a little of the history of Kurunegala to me! They told me that Kurunegala has been named after the Elephant rock which stands out in this city. 'Kurune' means tusker – an elephant with large tusks and 'gala' in Sinhalese means rock. This was once the royal capital in the history of our country – starting with the reign of King Parakramabahu III who transformed it into a beautiful city (1287-1293) After this King Buwanekabahu II (1293-1302) followed by King Parakramabahu IV (1302-1326) were the rulers. Kurunegala is known for its massive outcrop of rocks which have been named after the animals they resemble. According to legend, during a severe drought the animals threatened the water supply and as a punishment were turned into stone! The ones I was familiar with were the 'atha' elephant, and 'ibba' tortoise – but I know there were more animal rocks surrounding us! Kurunegala is an attractive regional town with a beautiful lake in the middle of the city.

Driving up to the house we were to occupy I was amazed to see this enormous rock that stood behind it and it was only then that I knew that this was the famous Atha Gala of Kurunegala! In front of the house across the road lay Ibba Gala – which was a flat rock with a slight incline on one side.

My father was appointed as the Office Assistant in Kurunegala. At that time Mr Herbert Tennakoon was the GA and there was also an Assistant Government Agent based in Kurunegala. The bungalow allocated to us had a garden on one side extending up a small rock which had steps cut into it and led up to a flat area where the Kachcheri was located. So, this was the office where my dad worked! His duties remained similar as before except that he didn't have any harbour visits like in Trinco. He had to supervise matters involving the Police and Legal administration and the General & Local Electoral procedures that took place within the District. He also had to pay regular circuit visits to the surrounding towns which came under the control of the main Government office in Kurunegala. He was also a Registrar of Marriages and I do recall some strange incidents which took place in this line of work! Like the time the young bride-to-be absolutely refused to marry the boy chosen for her and screamed and said she was NOT going to marry him and that was that! My dad worked through the entire evening to sort out this matter!

What strikes me now was the remarkable attitude my father had in regard to his position as OA. He kept very strictly to the rules of the Civil Service at that time. For example – he had an 'official car and an official driver' which he used for all his working projects; he also had a private car and driver for the family to use. We would go to school in the private car with our personal driver. But I recall an instance when the private car had broken down and my father refused to take us in the official car without the permission of the GA! He felt it was too early in the morning to disturb the GA and my sister and I had to walk to school that day! Fortunately, it wasn't too far and we got quite used to walking to and from school – and actually quite enjoyed it! So, this didn't bother us too much. However, another day when it rained heavily and the private car was again out of service and he couldn't get through to the GA, we had to miss school and stay at home! If he ever had to use the official driver or car for our own use, he would first pay the office the money due towards the petrol and driver's remunerations before actually using the driver and car! This was the regular manner in which the Civil Service functioned at that time – quite a contrast to the way governmental rules are observed today!

The house was quite different from the one at Trinco, being more British in its architectural design. It was on a higher level – at least seven or eight steps to get up to floor level unlike the one in Trinco which was just two steps off the ground. There was a spacious verandah which ran on four sides of the house. On one side we had a square table where we used to have our tiffin at 4.30 each evening – a custom so much endeared at that time and now completely unheard of! My mother, as I mentioned earlier, was an excellent cook and used to make not just sandwiches and perfect patties, but cupcakes, tarts, and also little buns filled either with minced meat or seeni sambol. We always had tea with these – plain tea in the pot served with milk and sugar served separately and in cups with saucers and cloth napkins. No paper serviettes and mugs at that time!!! The rest of the verandah had chairs and little side tables where friends used to sit and chat when they visited. Inside was a formal drawing room with sofas and matching chairs and large centre tables and side tables. Further in was the dining room and this was flanked on either side with bedrooms and bathrooms. When we left Trinco a foreign friend of ours gave us his refrigerator – (I think it was an Electrolux?) – as he was leaving the country and didn't intend taking it with him. This was our introduction to a fridge in our house! We took it with us to Kurunegala and had it in our dining room. So, it was easy to take the iced water and iced drinks straight from the fridge to the table!! From here we took it with us to Colombo and it went through several years with us during our Colombo days! I think it also had a freezer to make ice which was almost magical at that time!

Our 'Tiffin' verandah brings back some memories. I had a tiny toy piano with just fifteen keys, I think. I created some 'stick' friends from medium sized branch cuttings where I would attach some hairstyles made out of rough twine – so some were 'girls' and had long plaits (which my mother helped me to do!) and the 'boys' had the twine rolled on top and tied onto the stick! I would place them in a row and play some tunes on my piano and ask them to sing with me!! I really believed they were singing – of course it was I who was doing the real singing – shouting my head off!! The gardener's three daughters who were around my age would come home from time to time and spend the day with us. We would get together and have a great time playing with these stick friends! But none of my other friends knew about these imaginary creatures, so I used to hide my stick friends in our store room and only took them out when I was on my own or my three friends came over! When we left Kurunegala I gave all these to them and they were really happy to have them!

On one side there was a large bedroom leading onto another room and the toilet and bathroom (complete with bathtub and shower). This was the room my sister and I had to share. She used the extra room as her study room and I managed to get a part of it for my toys and other little treasures! After a few months, my 17 year old sister must have found it impossible to have me share a bedroom with her and moved out into her own room. I well recall how one night as I lay half asleep on my bed, I looked up to find a white sheeted something or another – I didn't know what! – leaning over me and swaying from side to side! With one huge scream I ran out of the room into my parents' room, which was just across the dining room. My parents woke up and were stunned to find me screaming there! They took me to their bed and my mum who was determined to sort this strange happening walked across to my sister's room and found her fast asleep. So, she told me I must have had a bad dream – there was no white covered thing in the room. But as I was so scared, they took me to their bed and from the next day arranged the guest room, which was adjoining theirs for me to use! So that was my new room but when a guest did visit, I would be only too happy to share my parents' bed! It was only years later that I realised who the white sheeted creature was!

The dining area opened out onto a wide long back verandah leading on to about four or five rooms on one side. My mother used the first one as her kitchen. The others were used for several purposes – there was the cook's kitchen and the rest of the rooms were used for their lodging and for storage purposes. We did see to it that one room on the corridor was used for the poultry who slept there at night and during the day wandered around the garden! The domestic workers and the gardeners had their rooms and bathrooms at the end of this corridor. Right at the back were two large open garages for the vehicles. The drivers had their quarters in this area. The garden was almost two acres and had various gradients – going up and then sloping down. The area in front of the house was flat land and had a range of beautiful flowering plants and attractive foliage. The surrounding garden had a wide range of trees and provided a wonderful playground for me and my imaginary friends! There were mango trees, kottang (Sri Lankan Almond Tree) trees and I loved picking up the fallen kottangs and smashing them open to eat the minute tasty kernel! There were a couple of enormous banyan trees – on whose roots I used to swing in my Tarzan games. There were several lawns – one circular lawn facing the porch edged by some flowering trees; a smaller triangular lawn facing the side entrance, also a large grass lawn on one side of the porch. A roadway circled this lawn and joined the path that led out of the gate. One side of the garden shared a boundary with the Kurunegala Town Hall. This was a small area and I well recall it had a gorgeous tree full of long leafy branches which had little pods at their ends and most of them were filled with some lovely small red seeds – 'maddichchi' seeds – reminding me of the Castle Street days. Another extended lawn stood facing the house and its boundary overlooked the roadway that led to the Town Hall. Beyond the roadway lay a large playing field, and further on, there were roads and buildings which were a part of the town.

The banyan tree I loved most was the one which stood on the right side of the entrance gate. My Tarzan antics were more developed now. My dad had a swing set up on one of the branches of the banyan tree and I would stand on this and swing high up getting into the clouds and then landing back on this planet! In addition to this, many of the thick dangling roots of the banyan came right down to ground level and I would swing on them imagining I was flying through some dangerous jungle hundreds of feet up in the air! A cousin had gifted us with a Golden Cocker-Spaniel puppy who we also named Kim, and although technically my sister was the rightful owner, I managed to persuade him to join me on my jaunts through the garden! He played many parts. In Tarzan he was the lion Jad-bal-ja and in my Roy Rogers games, he was Bullet the German Shepherd. We used to race around the garden hiding behind boulders, clambering up small rocks. Kim would be running furiously barking his head off and to add to the authenticity of the Tarzan games there were real monkeys roaming in our large garden. I reckon they were the Toque Macaque variety – brownish red in colour with a 'cap' of fur on their heads and lighter coloured underneath. They came from the wilderness of Elephant Rock and swung through the trees screeching and shaking the branches and creating a very realistic jungle scenario! In fact, I used to make a screeching call and they would all come out of wherever they were in answer to my call. I used to keep basins filled with water by the side of our back verandah and they would come right down to have a good drink. Once during our run-arounds, Kim and I were surrounded by perhaps ten to fifteen of these monkeys and we were not in the least frightened, although I had to keep a firm hand on Kim to prevent him from dashing out and grabbing them. But these games were not to last long because someone in my father's office had spotted this scene from the Kachcheri located above this area, and told my father to immediately call my mother and tell her that I should not under any circumstances play with the monkeys as they could get quite vicious at times! So, I was forbidden to play out my fantasy games and had to be content just running around the garden.

My dad loved walking around the garden and I loved accompanying him. There were some mounds of sand hills in the garden with holes on their sides, which my dad said were snake holes. He would take a stick and put it into a hole and I would have to guess whether there was a snake in it or not. To our surprise once a snake crept out looking startled of course. But my dad didn't get upset with this and just continued walking around while the snake slid through the grass into some secret corner!

We took special care of the poultry – they enjoyed one of the rear verandah rooms to themselves and were let out each morning to frisk around the enormous garden. Come evening and they would dutifully return to their room. They grew old with us, those chickens; one or two went blind or lame and I would have to 'feed' them by carrying their little plates of food right up to their beaks. Each of them had a name and I would sit by them and talk to them while they ate. As time went by they gradually died of old age so that when we had to leave Kurunegala there weren't any left. I wonder if there were, whether I would have insisted we bring them to Colombo?! A friend brought us two young female turkeys to add to our poultry collection! These two had to be trained on how to get around the garden and not leave the property and also to get back in time for their night sleep. This was quite a task as they were totally unfamiliar with this routine. So, the boy in charge had plenty to do and I took over at times to give him a rest. When they didn't turn up by evening, we would have to go searching for them – all around the large garden which was quite exhausting to say the least. Then we would suddenly spot them in some corner and take them back to their room at the back of our house. After several weeks they did fall into the routine – much to our relief. They would strut around the garden and come over for their food and water and then they would perch on the water barrel looking quite smart!

We set up a badminton court on one of the side lawns. We had great fun playing badminton almost every evening – my dad, my sister and myself. Sometimes we asked friends to make a foursome. I wondered why no one particularly wanted to be my partner – all these serious teenage and older badminton players – maybe at almost nine I wasn't quite the expert. Just opposite our house was the District Judge's bungalow – again a large house with a rambling garden. We were close friends of the Wijewardenas – Uncle Earle and Aunty Merle – they had two sons Gihan and Ajit. Gihan was at the Peradeniya University and was much older than we were, but Ajit was around my sister's age and was boarded at Royal College in Colombo. He would come to Kurunegala for the holidays and he would come over to our place to play badminton – of course when he realised he had to partner me he was very reluctant to play! I was very friendly with Uncle and Aunty and used to pop over to their place sometimes just to say 'Hello' to them. One day while I was doing my usual evening stand at our gate, I saw Uncle Earle walking towards me – we waved to each other and then he told me that there were two beautiful ladies elegantly dressed who had come to their place searching for our house as they wanted to meet my father. So, could my mother come and bring them over. I immediately ran in and told my mother about this and she came out and met Uncle Earle and asked him the name of these visitors.

"I don't know – but they want you to come and take them to your place so please do – we'll wait on the verandah for you." was his reply.

"Could you tell them to just come across to our place?"

"I did – but they were silent and looked glum – so I told them I would ask you to come over and take them."

Of course, my mother went back into our house and called my dad who hadn't a clue as to who these 'elegantly dressed ladies' were!! Well, my mother tidied herself up – and got me to tidy up (as she called it) and then we both walked over to the Wijewardena's house across the road. When we got there Uncle Earle greeted us on the verandah and then pointed to the far end –

"There they are – the important visitors to see you." We looked around and couldn't see any 'elegantly dressed ladies' when Uncle Earl pointed out to the far end of the verandah – and we couldn't believe our eyes! Why the 'two important visitors' were none other than our two white turkeys – seated on two chairs looking quite stately and pompous! They flicked their eyes as soon as they saw us and I asked them to get down from the chairs and come back home with me – of course they didn't respond immediately but must have spotted the stern note in my voice and then jumped off the chairs and followed me back to our house. It all ended with a good laugh by all of us!

My dad meanwhile had come home after work and the domestics had told him the story about the important lady visitors who were coming in from the opposite house. He was walking towards our gate when we came in laughing, with our turkeys traipsing along.

"Where are the visitors?" he asked.

"These are the visitors," we replied.

Much laughter again – only the turkeys were silent and stared at me with deep concern. Had we all gone mad or what?

There was a wide drain of about three feet and about two feet deep which ran right through the rear part of the garden –just below the area where there were the steps cut into the rock going up to the Kachcheri. Elephant rock stood towering behind it. There was a pond on the top of Elephant Rock and during heavy rains the water used to gush down the rock and flow in a torrent through the drain that ran through our garden. To my great delight the water also brought in some of the fish from the pond! I used to enjoy just playing around in the water and feeling the fish swim by, nibbling at my feet! When friends used to come over to spend the day we would sit here and enjoy keeping our feet in the water.

Lorni and I attended Holy Family Convent in Kurunegala. This was located in the centre of the town. My dad used to send us by car to school but when he couldn't do this my sister and I used to walk to school, as it wasn't too far from where we lived. I well remember the wonderful clock tower located in the centre of the town from where several roadways branched out in different directions. The tower was built in 1922 in memory of soldiers who fought in World War I. But, in the year 1945, it was dedicated to the officers who died in the Second World War. We got used to walking to school and back and our guideline was the clock tower – it was almost halfway and I could gauge how long we would take to get to our destination.

Holy Family Convent had a different order of nuns and was a bigger school than the one in Trinco. Now I was eight plus. I went into a class that did all their work in Sinhala. I couldn't manage this as I had been in the English stream in Trinco. So, I was sent for special lessons with a lovely teacher, Mrs Baldsing, where I could work in English. The next year I was put into a class which did their work in English so I fitted in well. It didn't take me too long to make friends. The school became a haven of fun for me for not only did we do our studies but also learn to sing, dance, play games, and regularly took part in school concerts. I recall the Olupaliyawa family who lived next to the Convent where we used to go after school and have plain tea and vades which we thoroughly enjoyed! Then we used to stand at the gate and watch out for the very large green car which came to collect our friend Chuli de Saram and her sisters from school. I well recall Mirabel Arnolda who taught us dancing, and how I absolutely loved her classes! This was my introduction to ballet and I continued to love ballet even when I was older. Her sisters Annabel and Christobel also attended the Convent. I remember how she brought a hula hoop from Colombo and we were totally captivated by this! We took these large 'rings' put them over our heads down to our waists and turned this way and that and discovered how the hula hoop just swayed around with us! The Convent also was very adept at promoting the Arts among the students and I well recall them staging some excerpts from a classical opera - Verdi's *Il Trovatore* – where my sister Lorni who was an excellent singer, played an important role. In this way HFC gave us many opportunities to sharpen our artistic skills.

Soon I was in my own little group and we had good times together apart from being in school. We used to have 'spend the days' at each other's homes and this usually took place on a Saturday or on a holiday. I never revealed the imaginary games I played with my dog for fear they would laugh at me! With them I played regular games like hide and seek or hopscotch. My father taught me board games like draughts and carom and we also played thayam-chonal –totally unheard of now!! So, these were very much part of my social skills with my friends.

I used to visit Roshni Gunasekera (she had a brother named Tilak) and spend the day with her – we had wonderful times playing games, singing and dancing and eating all sorts of delicacies! We also visited Chulangani de Saram whom we called 'Ungi' (now we call her Chuli! – the same Chuli with the big green car!) and I well remember their lovely large house and garden. I would often dash across to Jenny Tennakoon's place which was located just above our house and on one side of the Kachcheri. Her father was the Government Agent, Herbert Tennakoon and her mother was a really beautiful lady who to me was Aunty Norma. They lived in a majestic house called the *Maligawa* – which was really large and very elegant and the garden was vastly spread out on every side with rocks overlooking some of the boundaries. Aunty Norma was a dynamic lady and she began an association for the ladies where they met at her place regularly and organised various community projects. She was also excellent at entertaining and often had parties for her friends. Jenny had a sister Hemi who was older than we were and a brother Gihan who was a boarder at Trinity College, Kandy.

There was no Methodist Church in Kurunegala and we used to have family gatherings twice a month in the home of a Methodist family where the pastor from Kandy would come down to conduct a prayer service for us. So, we regularly attended the Anglican Church and I went to the Sunday School while Lorni was a staunch member of the Youth Fellowship. Lorni joined a group for Bible Study at Rev Dassanayake's – (he was the local Vicar of the Anglican Church) house and I used to go with her to play in their garden!

Kurunegala also had a vibrant social circle. My family also had their own special friends and we used to visit them on weekends mainly in the evenings just for a chat. There were the Casinaders, and the Buells (Uncle Sam and Aunty Chloe), the Jansens – Rex and Patrick are the names I recall. The Moonemalles – Lakshman, Kingsley and Rosemarie. Kingsley was in and out of our house – Lakshman we hardly ever saw and Rosemarie was the very pretty sister who was boarded in a school out of Kurunegala. The other names that come to mind were Norman and Rosemarie Jobsz, and the Police guys Leslie Kodithuwakku and Lakshman Perera. The other friends we regularly kept in touch with were the Jayasinghes – Ian was a friend and Manel was my classmate and Lathika in a higher class, the Frasers – Jeanne was Lorni's classmate and Heather was a little older than I. My sister's school buddies were also Indrani Heart, Jean Fraser and Stephanie Andradi but she also had her own group of friends from some of the names mentioned here. She was also friendly with Kingsley Moonemale, Ian Jayasinghe and Patrick Jansen and used to go to the cinema with them! The three guys called themselves The Three Musketeers and when Lorni joined she called them the Four Musketeers! The Three Ms would always bring Lorni back safely home after the film much to my parents' relief! Therese Batcho was my classmate and I'll never forget her because when we left Kurunegala I had a mynah who used to come to our place and stay in a little meshed box for the night (in the poultry room). We used to open it up for him during the day and he would fly around the garden and then come back to stay with us! He became quite a chatterbox and when Therese used to come home she always spent time talking to him! We were really worried about what would happen to him once we left Kurunegala – because we knew we couldn't take him to Colombo. Fortunately, much to our relief, Therese was only too happy to take him over! There were the Lallyetts – Uncle Gordon used to be a planter at Labookelli Estate and moved to Kurunegala when he retired. He lived with his wife – Aunty Rosemary, and daughters Anne and Pat who attended the Convent – so we became close friends. They had built a modern looking two level house just outside the busy urban area and I would love to stand on their large balcony and gaze at the trees and people and traffic on the roads below.

I remember visiting the Pattersons. There was Uncle Spencer, Aunty Beryl, Babs and Spencer. We seated ourselves on their broad verandah and sipped cool drinks and ate delicious shorteats! I will never forget the first time we visited them. Aunty kept looking at the clock on the wall in the dining room and mumbling that, "Donny had not returned as yet." We took it that this was the third child – perhaps a young boy? "He should be back by now surely!" Aunty muttered aloud. My mother asked, "Where's he gone? Somewhere far?" "No – just to the pictures – he has to take a bus back." We used to refer to the movies as 'pictures' then. She sat talking to us when suddenly she rose to her feet. "Ah there he is! Come darling – why are you so late – I was getting worried about you." A white dog skipped in jauntily and jumped all over her returning her hugs and kisses with greetings in his own doggie way. So, this was Donny – and he had come back by bus? She explained – "Oh yes he knows all the bus drivers and they stop here to pick him up and drop him off in town – where he does his rounds – sometimes ending up at a show – and then he hops a bus there and gets back to us." It sounded so simple and routine – but needless to say we were absolutely flabbergasted when we heard this!

My mother was an old friend of the Bevans – Uncle Cecil, Aunty Edna, Barbara, Megan and David. Aunty Edna was a music teacher so I went to her for piano lessons. When I got there early, Uncle Cecil would always ask me whether I wanted to play in the garden while I waited rather than just sit down on a chair on the verandah. Of course, this is what I wanted to do so off I went into their large garden and ran around talking to myself and inventing all kinds of imaginary games with the garden characters – ranging from the chameleons who changed colour and created a magic world, to the birds who flew around and perched on the branches of the surrounding trees. The problem was that when the class was ready to commence and I was asked to get to the piano I was too involved in my own world and would hide to escape the shouts of Uncle Cecil. When he finally found me he sternly ordered me to get to the class at once! One day during this sequence he said "The whole problem with you is that you are like a *kurukunda*". I was so afraid when he said this that I kept silent with the fear that throbbed in my chest. When I returned home I burst into tears and my mum wanted to know what this was all about, and when I told her the story all they did was laugh – my dad and Lorni were there too! They explained that a 'kurukunda' – was the local name for millipede – (although they resemble insects they are classified as Arthropods) it was a creature that walked and walked and then turned around in a circle when it wanted to sleep I think? It was only a fun way of telling me that I was running around too much! I really loved playing the piano but my mother was still grieving over the loss of my brother, who was a brilliant pianist, and refused to have a piano in our house. She cared for us as a family with the utmost devotion but looking back I was very much aware that to her last days she never got over the sadness of the absence of my brother.

The Pouliers were also dear friends of ours – Uncle Eric, Aunty Hilda, Betty, Eric, Fanny and Harry. Aunty Hilda was related to my mother and we often visited one another's homes. Fanny and I were in the same class in school so we became very close friends and still are. The Pouliers too lived slightly out of the busy areas of the town in a single level house with an enormous open ended garden. Sometimes on a Friday evening after school I would go with Fanny to her place, play around and have a sumptuous tea – and my parents would then come over to pick me up late in the evening – and also have a chat with them! I well recall that Fanny used to travel in a buggy cart sometimes – otherwise her dad would drop her off in his car. I loved going back with her in the buggy. My grave concern however was that the driver smacked the bull really hard sometimes to get him to move faster. This used to really upset me and once I actually tried to climb into the driver's seat and screamed at him for being so cruel to the poor bull! Of course, I didn't get a chance, for he just screamed back at me to get back into the cart before I fell off and broke my bones! When we reached Fanny's house he complained to her mother about my behaviour and I was warned never again to shout at him. Of course, I never got to know what the bull thought of all this!

Then we used to visit the Daniels and their relatives on their vast estate where they would have a campfire and barbeque dinner. There were Uncle Ernie and Aunty Doreen and Dianne Lockhart, and Carol and Sonia Daniels were all friends of our family. We used to often visit the de Zilwas, and their daughters Moira and Tania were in the same school as we were. We enjoyed getting together and singing all the old songs and clapping until our hands were numb! The Jayasunderas were also good friends and we used to visit each other regularly.

My classmate Edna Wells lived on an estate just outside Kurunegala – I think it was called *Clovis* estate. Her dad Vernon was a real wild life fan and on one of his jungle trips had been attacked by a leopard who had torn off his ear. I would gaze at Uncle Vernon's face which had a scar on one side and no ear. I couldn't imagine such a terrible thing happening to anyone. I would get him to repeat the story of how this happened every time I went there! I would spend a weekend with them sometimes and enjoy myself in their large upstairs house which had a spacious balcony overlooking acres of forest !

I still manage to meet up with some of these old friends. I am in touch with Roshni, Chuli, Jenny, Fanny, and Manel and meet up with Dianne, when she visits Sri Lanka from England.

Relatives and friends from Colombo and other parts of the country also visited regularly. I well recall again how my cousin Allister and our family friend Gamini used to visit us so often. Sometimes when we opened the front doors early morning we would find Gamini fast asleep on the 'haansi putuwa' on the verandah! He had come on the night train and arrived early morning! I still recall my cousin Margot and her son Shane coming over quite often from Colombo. Shane was a couple of years younger than I was – so maybe around five at the time. To escape playing with him I would dash into the garden and climb my favourite frangipani tree which stood right in front of the verandah. It didn't take me two minutes to clamber up its branches and get to a high point of the tree. From there I could see little Shane running around shouting my name. I would stay absolutely still and quiet and wait like this until I heard him going into the house to see whether I was there!

Climbing Atha Gala became a frequent pastime for us. When we had a free evening, we would look at one another and then make the snap decision to climb the rock. There were steps cut into the rock and after a long haul we were on top. The view from here was stupendous – buildings and people looked smaller than ants below. A lovely Buddhist Temple stood right on the summit and was a place perfect for meditation and prayer. There was a lovely pond with some colourful fish swimming around – this was the pond that used to overflow when it rained and flowed down into the large drain in our garden! Often, we would take some snacks and sit at the top and have a treat! Coming down as always was a tricky business but we would laugh and slide and edge our way to this side and that and finally reach the bottom! I remember how often the Pouliers would climb this rock with us! Of course, we had a basket of snacks made by Aunty Hilda and my mother to give us a treat while we did our climb!

Just opposite our house stood a flat stretch of rock which was called Ibba Gala (Tortoise rock). This didn't need any special climbing skills – and it was fun to just run along on the rock –so when friends came over we would have fun just running along the rock!

The lake in Kurunegala was another important feature in its landscape. This was a large man-made reservoir built by ancient kings. Our treat was to go for a walk round the lake. Almost two miles I'd imagine but we did it with gusto and delight. Of course, here again my sister would leap on to her bike and cycle around the lake with her friends while we jogged along! It was great fun to gaze into the water and look on the side where large houses were embedded far inside vast gardens. We had friends living in some of them and often we would just drop in for a chat. Dropping in on friends was an accepted thing at that time, unlike now where one has to almost make an appointment to meet up with someone!

The family outings were to the Bathalagoda and Ibbagamuwa Tanks – these were built to supply water to this area. We would often drive down to these places and have a picnic – gulping down my mother's tasty eats and homemade drinks! As a part of his official duties as Office Assistant my dad would go on circuit to neighbouring small towns and we would often accompany him, enjoying the trip and savouring yet another experience of the rural culture of the area. We always took our Cocker-Spaniel Kim with us and often at the resthouses, where we stopped over for a meal, the waiters would serve him his food on a plate on the floor, all very neatly set out – rice in the centre and curries all around! Kim would look at it puzzled at what this concoction was and look up at my mother who would pick up the plate and mix it all up and then set it back on the floor where he would happily guzzle it bit by bit.

During the few years we were in Kurunegala we visited the cinema regularly. Every Thursday was a change of show and my dad unfailingly got us together and we walked down our short cut which was a small winding road to the cinema. More often than not we would spot Donny curled up on a chair and after the show would see him run out to the bus-stand which stood close to the cinema, and climb into a bus – that would take him home! The amazing thing was that the conductors on the busses all knew Donny and they would greet him when he got into the bus! When a film ran for over a week then of course we had to take a break until a new one came in!

We used to visit Colombo quite often, for here too my father had to deal with various Government officials in connection with his job as Office Assistant in Kurunegala. We would stay with my mother's sister and family (mentioned later in this story) who lived down Sri Saranankara Road, Dehiwala. I recall how when Donovan Andree produced "Holiday on Ice" we came down to Colombo to see it. Even now I think it was a remarkable show especially to be done in a day and time when technology wasn't anywhere near where it is today. I guess everything for the show was done by hand – Donovan, being the showman he was, had organised a complete ice-skating rink to be created on which the artistes gave a fantastic performance. What puzzles me is how they kept the ice from melting in our very tropical hot weather.

I recall making several trips to Kandy from Kurunegala. I reckon my father had to attend to some work in the government offices in Kandy. We would go on a Friday

Daddy buying ice cream in Kurunegala.

Lorni dressed up for an Opera she was singing in with me in my ballet butterfly costume in the concert, Kurunegala.

Lorni before going to the opera produced by the convent in Kurunegala.

Wearing my butterfly ballet costume in Kurunegala.

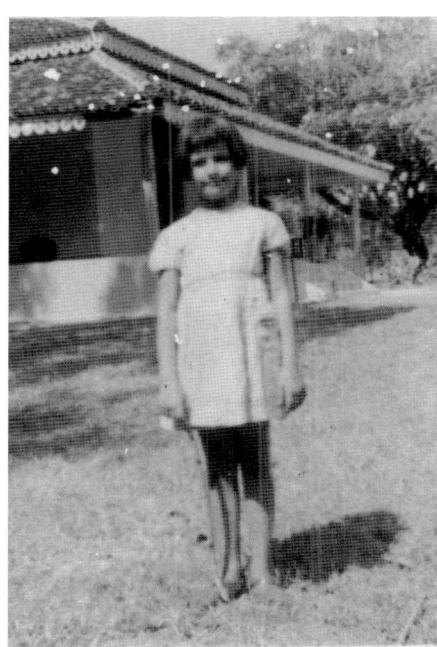

Me in Kurunegala on the side lawn.

Family photo with Lorni, Daddy wearing his coronation medal, Mummy and myself, photo taken on a trip to Colombo around 1955.

night and get back on Sunday evening. I had an uncle who lived in Kandy, Dr. Roy Peterson, a very well-known doctor at the time. He lived in a lovely spacious house on Peradeniya Road next to Girls' High School. What I remember most about Uncle Roy's place was that he had a lovely rocking chair on the verandah and I would love to sit on it and rock up and down! He was married to my dad's sister Rachel and they had one son Eric, who was a planter on an upcountry tea estate. Later Eric married Bunty and they had three children Paula, Robert and Jeremy. While daddy was at work my mother, sister and I would go around Kandy, walking around the lake and roaming the streets. Having lived in Kandy for many years (I was born there remember!) my mum knew the ins and outs of all the streets. We visited some friends of hers – the McGills. Aunty Edna was the chief Nurse at Dr Anthonisz's medical clinic and she had a son called Arthur. During the Perahera season we used to watch the parade from the verandah of her house. Sometimes we would visit their old friends – the Van Reyks, Vanderwerts, Ludowykes and the Moldrich family. Sunday evening would come and we would take off for our home in Kurunegala.

Only too soon came the time for us to leave Kurunegala – my father's term was over and he was being sent to a Government office in Colombo. I was extremely sad to leave our lovely house and garden and all my wonderful friends. Where would I ever get a garden like this to play all my lovely games and climb all those gorgeous trees? Climbing the rocks and walking round the lake –

the marvellous times I had in school – all that was being taken away from my life. My eyes filled with tears each time I thought of all these experiences and I now had to face the challenge of living in a new place, meeting new people and making new friends. My dad's date of appointment in Colombo was in mid-October which was in the middle of our school term. Our good friends, the Jayasunderas, very kindly offered to let me stay with them until the term was over. It was the first time in my life that I would be separated from my family, but strangely enough I was not too concerned about this as I was very fond of their family. I fitted in perfectly with them. Uncle was a well-known Ayurvedic practitioner in Kurunegala. Aunty was constantly around me – seeing that I had everything I needed! They had four daughters and one son – Sujatha, Sepalika, Sunethra, Lala and the one boy Sanath – all wonderful loving people – who took great care of me! Aunty was an expert cook and made some very tasty dishes! I walked with the girls to and from school each day and the weekends were spent chatting and visiting friends! The sisters were good pianists and sang well so I had a great time listening to some really good music and singing along with them! My family meanwhile had taken a flat in Colpetty – very tiny compared to our recent abodes outstation! My dad used to come down occasionally and take me to Colombo for the weekend and then bring me back on Sunday evening. The Colombo house was like a doll's house to me – the novelty of living in a two bedroomed flat was interesting in a certain kind of way!

Finally, the day came for me to leave Kurunegala and although I was happy to reunite with my family, I was sad to leave a life I knew I would never see again. I would never forget the wonderful days we spent there. Still, I had to move on and I did. Once in Colombo, I was happy to be with my family and my doggie of course!

PART FOUR

COLOMBO DAYS – EARLY AND LATER!

COLOMBO DAYS – Early childhood

These are memories I have after my brother died and we used to visit friends and relatives while we were in Colombo and also when we used to come down from Trinco and Kurunegala – which we did often, as my dad was in regular contact with the Senior Officers of the Civil Service who were based in Colombo. We always stayed with relatives so we were constantly visiting aunts and uncles and their families.

I loved going to my uncle's house down Elibank Road – off Dickman's Road, Colombo. This was my mother's brother Eldred Cecil Herft – called Uncle Eldie by us – who had qualified as a Civil Engineer in Scotland and married a lady from Austria – Leopoldine Skrovny – to us she was Auntie Dina. They didn't have children and loved having all of us around! We would go there probably once every two or three weeks. They had a lovely large house and a rambling garden where we could all get together and play. Most of my cousins (on my mother's side) would be there, so it was great fun. The garden had a low parapet wall surrounding its boundary and we would love to stand against it or even on it, and watch the world go by!

The grownups would sit on the verandah or around the dining table and indulge in sipping cups of tea and soft drinks and munching on patties and cake to accompany the natter. We children, after gorging the tasty short eats and having our tumblers filled with drinks used to dash outside to play in the garden.

Being among the younger group of my cousins I was often teased (in a fun kind of way) by the older lot. I never forget the times when we visited Uncle Eldie and Auntie Dina and stood by the wall or sat on the wall gazing out at the roadway – when suddenly my cousins would point out in the distance, "Look – there they're coming!" And when I looked I could see the tall figures of men walking down the road – dressed in baggy trousers, long shirts, their heads draped in turbans. It was more like a march down the road rather than a walk. I knew who these were because my cousins had told me that these were the 'Baaiyas'. I couldn't get over the fact that they were so tall and big and asked my cousins how this was. They answered that they were so big because they used to swallow children – especially small children on walls! Their gaze seemed to fix on me in a way which made me feel that these giants would make me their next victim! In a state of total panic, I would leap off the wall screaming, then dash inside and grab my mother (who would be sipping her tea) and burst into tears. This became such a common practice that no one really took me seriously except my mother who held me close and told me not to be frightened that she wouldn't let anyone swallow me up. When I looked into her grey-green eyes I knew that one look from her (when she was angry her eyes would develop a very pale green glint which could be quite a threatening look to say the least) and those giants would flee the scene, so after a few minutes I was brave enough to continue with my games!

We took it in turn to host and visit our relatives so every weekend was an adventure! My mother's sister Esme was married to Carl Bartholomeusz and lived down Mary's Road, Wellawatte. Their children were Allister who was in his late teens at the time, daughters Carol, Myrna, Ione, and Heidi who was a few months younger than I was. My late brother Jim was very close to Allister and we felt an irreplaceable gap in our lives when we visited their place after Jim's death. As always, we would be munching short eats and sipping Ginger Beer, Necto or Portello while we played in their garden and sometimes we just sat on their verandah and sang our favourites at that time! We also visited my mum's sister Aunty Dona who was married to Leslie Campbell – they had one daughter Jeanne – lived down Sri Saranankara Road, Dehiwala in one of the houses belonging to Dr R. L. Spittel's Housing Scheme – (this was the house we later occupied). Mum's brother Annesley Herft and his wife Carmen lived down de Kretser Place, Bambalapitiya and we enjoyed visiting them too – I remember their sons Piers and Gavin and daughter Romayne. Then, there was Uncle Orville, Aunty Gwen and my cousins Deanna and Ingrid. Uncle Vyville and his family – my cousins Judy, Warner and Wendy. Aunty Thelma – mum's sister – married to Alex Hepponstall – children were Lausanne and Ian. My cousin Margot and her baby son Shane lived with Uncle Eldie and Aunty Dina. Margot's late mother Ena was my mother's sister and they lived with my grandparents in Negombo. Aunty Ena died at childbirth when Margot was born. The legend goes that many people who lived in that house claimed they saw the ghost of a pretty young lady who walked through the house whenever there was a baby in it. She never did any harm to anyone but just walked around the place and then disappeared! After my grandparents died Margot and Shane stayed with Uncle Eldie and Aunty Dina at Elibank Road. We saw Shane growing up – used to call him Pudu when he was a kid! Shane became a very close friend and we still keep in touch and love talking about the old times! We always kept in touch with Margot who was a very talented dancer, both in ballet and modern dancing. After some years she married Murad Uduman (who held a senior post in one of the Banks) and they moved to their own house. They had a son called Sohrab and lived down Kinross Avenue and we used to see them very often. In my teen years after my mother had passed away and I stayed with my dad at Charlemont Road Margot helped us greatly by sending us our dinner on week days – this saved me the trouble of having to get back home after work and make our dinner! She was an excellent cook and also had a heart of gold! I will never forget how kind she was to us. After this they moved to London where Murad got a senior posting in a bank there.

That was my mother's side – now for my father's! There were five boys and six girls – some of them died at a very young age. My dad's sisters whom I recall were Rachel who married Dr Roy Peterson – a well-known doctor in Kandy – they had one son Eric. Phyllida (called Auntie Phylla by us) and Queenie were teachers at Ladies College – they lived in a large house at Castle Street (referred to earlier in this story); Zillah was married to Bertram Pollocks – a popular cricketer in his day. Uncle Bertie – as we used to call him – was first married to dad's sister Ray and they had two children Douglas and Rita; then Ray died and he married the younger sister Zillah whose children were Herbert, Brian, Earle and Joyce. It was a common custom at that time that when a man's wife died he married an unmarried sister in that family – perhaps this was to keep the family together! My dad's brother Neville was an eminent Pastor of the Dutch Reformed Church. He had qualified at Princeton University – a rare accomplishment at that time. Daddy had another brother Hugh, who was a Lawyer (Proctor) and married to Queenie (née Schoorman) and lived down Frances Road, Wellawatte. They had no children and were always ready to provide a home for their relatives. The house at Castle Street became quite empty after Aunt Phylla died. Cousin Douglas had gone to Australia, the others living there had also left, we too had moved out – so it was just my Aunt Queenie, her adopted helper Dinah and doggie Tony who were there. My uncle Hugh and his wife (also named Queenie) stayed in a spacious house at Frances Road, Wellawatte, and they asked the three of them to come over and live with them. So, there were now two Queenies at Frances Road! Because the two names used to get mixed up we used to refer to dad's sister as 'Sister Queenie'! My cousin Rita and her daughter Loretta also stayed there for a short time. A house full of relatives!!

1955 – NEW ROAD (Now called Lower Bagatelle Road)

I was just over ten years old when we began our second round of living in Colombo!

Our first home in Colombo after our stay in Trinco and Kurunegala was located at New Road Colpetty – now called Lower Bagatelle Road. A very residential area and very convenient for me to get to school (Methodist College, Colpetty), for my dad to get to work – he was the Administrative Officer in the Health Ministry which was located at the former Parliament building (Galle Face), and for Lorni to go for her secretarial classes and also to work later at Walker Sons. My dad had a new car at this time – a Hillman Minx CN7971!

We had the ground floor of a flat which reminded me of a doll's house – everything was absolutely tiny! The bathroom was so narrow you could hardly spread your arms while having a shower. The bedrooms had hardly any space for clothes' cupboards or dressing tables. The dining and sitting areas were all in one room where you could hardly move your chair. The kitchen was like a part of a corridor where you couldn't turn around once you were inside!

So now at ten-plus I was in Colombo and my parents' main objective was to get me into Methodist College, which was (and still is!) a well-established school. I had to do an entrance test and will always remember being taken by my mother to meet the Principal – Miss Grace Robins. After a short pleasant chat my mum was told to sit outside while I was taken to a room where a teacher gave me some question papers which I had to answer. I read them very carefully and wrote down the answers as clearly as I could. My head was in a whirl and my hands shook as I went over and handed them to the teacher in charge! Later that week my heart leapt with joy when I was told that I had been accepted as a student at Methodist College!

I was quite thrilled about this but at the same time found it quite challenging! What would the new girls be like? What would the new teachers be like? What would they say when they discovered that I had come from an outstation school? Would the work be more complicated in a Colombo school? My entire being was teeming with worries and my parents had to convince me that everything was going to be just fine!

I was also adjusting to our current neighbourhood and I was overjoyed when the girl who lived just opposite our house, Pat Geddes, came over to meet me and told me she went to Methodist College! My fears melted and I now looked forward to going to my new school! At least now I knew one student! My mother got an MC uniform from her and made me a couple of them so I could go on the first day suitably dressed.

A wonderful beginning to what has left me with many happy memories of my school days at MC!

My cousin Margot and her husband Murad Uduman lived in a large flat almost opposite our place at New Road. My little cousin Shane was also there so I felt happy to be so close to them. Margot was an expert dancer and had ballroom dancing classes at her place a couple of times each week. My sister who was also a very good dancer used to join them! We loved to stand outside and watch them waltzing and jiving! Then suddenly one day some heavy curtains were drawn during the classes so that no one from the outside could see the dancing in progress! – but of course, we could hear the wonderful music being played for them!

It was Pat who gave me the name 'Ant' – she said there was no point in having so many syllables to a name – for instance she was Patricia but was called Pat! So, the name stuck and still I have friends who call me Ant! I became close friends with Pat (still am!) – she had two sisters Christine and Mignonne and two brothers Cecil and Ian. Ian was a part of our group and Pat also introduced me to the kids in the neighbourhood and I was happy to be a part of the team! We used to often play hopscotch on the road in front of our house, with Pat, her brother Ian and one or two other kids who lived around us. We also played rounders and then we would get back to our homes and our usual routine! Our lane was on the seaside and we walked down where there was a rail-track which we had to cross to get to the tiny beach and the sea! We loved watching the trains go tooting and chunking along. There were rocks by the shore and just a few feet below was a narrow stretch of beach and the sea. It was a treat for us to go down and enjoy the waves!

We used to also visit some of the residents at New Road who were very friendly. We had Oosha de Livera living in front of our house – she had a little son called Rohan (Goonetilleke) who used to join in all our games.

Our small group decided that at Christmas we should do a concert to raise funds for ourselves – we couldn't wait to go to the ice cream shop and have a scoop! We turned our garage into a theatre. There was no door to the garage and my mother fixed a curtain across the front section which we drew open when the show started! We had a hat collection instead of tickets and one of us stood at our gate taking in whatever contribution was offered! Pat and I had planned to organise some songs, we also did some ballet dances. I well remember how little Rohan sang *Wizard of Oz* but didn't know when he should stop! Finally, we started clapping and I told him this was a sign that he should stop and leave the stage!!! – which he did very reluctantly! He also dressed up in his 'grasshopper' costume which he had used in a school concert and did his dance, with fingers pointing upward with every hop he did! Wonderful! The little girls in our group did some dance acts and then we all joined together and sang some popular songs as a grand finale to the famous performance!!

We were quite surprised at the number of neighbours who were present and we had to borrow chairs (from them of course!!!) to provide seats for them! At the end of it, we were absolutely thrilled that we had enough money for quite a stack of ice creams! My dad took us all piled up in his little car to the ice cream shop round the corner and we all picked and chose our favourites and went back home tired but very happy at the success of our first concert!

Then Pat and her family moved to a house that was right at the end of the next lane. Just beyond on the other side of the lane was a palatial mansion called *Mumtaz Mahal*. The land it occupied extended from the Galle Road right up to the railtrack near the beach! Later on, this was turned into the Parliamentary Speaker's residence. It had a large boundary wall which edged one side of the lane where Pat and her family now lived. Pat and Ian used to climb up this 10 foot wall and jump – onto our side of course! – just to see how far out they could jump! I remember going with them once and being totally swamped by the whole idea of this – for how was I to climb this wall and then jump onto a very uneven stony surface on the road? No, I just couldn't do it – so I was totally out of this game! We used to love walking along the Galle Road and stopping at the gates of *Mumtaz Mahal* and wish we could just run in for a peek! But it was well guarded at the gates and our wishes just flew out of the window!

I also remember how Pat, Ian and I used to walk along the Galle Road to the Junior Sunday School at the Methodist Church, Colpetty. A very sweet lady called Cuckoo Fonseka was in charge of the Junior Section of the Sunday School and her sister Doris was in charge of the higher level. We did a lot of singing and listened to Bible stories and also had to colour biblical drawings on sheets of paper which were handed out to us! We were allowed to take these back home. I well recall how one day we were late to leave for Sunday School and decided to do a small tour of the area and skip Sunday School! We walked down the various roads that surrounded us and got quite lost as to where exactly we were. After about two hours of roaming around in the hot sun we managed to find our way back home. Of course, we were so flaked out when we got home that our parents knew at once that something weird had happened! So, we had to confess the story. My parents – particularly my mother, was totally mad at me, and I had to face severe consequences for my irresponsible conduct! After that my dad used to drive us to Sunday School and we used to walk back home after it was over – with the drawing sheets as proof!

A favourite pastime of the family when we were young was to visit the Galle Face Green, go to the edge and gaze at the sea, fly kites during the kite season in April and go to either Pagoda Tea Room, Elephant House, or Fountain Café for a much loved ice cream cone!! We would also see movies regularly – we didn't have TV at the time – so all the favourite films would be screened in the cinemas – Liberty, Majestic, Regal, Rio or Savoy. The number of seats was very limited in comparison to today's super cinemas!

Even though I had great times at New Road we found the flat too small and decided to move to a larger place. Our next move one year later was to a slightly larger place at de Fonseka Road, Colombo 5. I was extremely sad to leave Pat and Ian and all my other friends – but the time had come – so I had to go with the family!

1956 – DE FONSEKA ROAD

This was a larger flat belonging to the Weeraratnes. Mrs Weeraratne owned a very beautiful walauwwa style house which was set in a large garden. She had built a two storeyed flat on one side of the house which she used to rent out. This was the flat we occupied. We were on the ground floor and in the one above us we had various families moving in and out from time to time. I recall a German couple who were very friendly with us. The lady couldn't speak English and we knew no German so conversations were rather complicated and sometime became quite confused! Like the time she came down shouting that there was somebody running all over her bedroom, must be a 'kollagog' a 'kollagog' – she looked terrified and was begging of us to help her. Only my mum and I were at home and I being the brave one actually took a broom upstairs to kill the intruder. My mind was racing – what on earth did 'kollagog' mean in German? A thief? A murderer? A – what? My mother followed me also armed with a wire brush – and was praying to the dear Lord to protect us from whatever was going to attack us. When we reached her floor there didn't seem to be anyone around. Could he be hiding somewhere? In the cupboard? Behind the door? In the bathroom? Then suddenly we heard a scream, "Here here here…." Turning around we spotted our friend pointing to something on the arm of the sofa. It was a cockroach! I managed to smash it with the broom and we took it away with a piece of paper. The 'kollagog' was killed – our friend was saved! She came over and hugged me. "Danke danke danke." We had saved her from this horrible monster. What a calamity! Of course, I was pleased; I had come out as a brave young girl although I did feel sad for the cockroach☹.

After that we had Eileen and Cliffy Ernst upstairs. Cliffy used to travel on a motorbike and also had a car for long trips. Eileen was an expert cook and often had us upstairs for tiffin. So, between my mother's excellent tiffins and Aunty Eileen's, we did enjoy a great deal of tasty delicacies! We kept in touch with them for many years and used to often visit them in later years when they moved to their house in Bandarawela. We used to stop over for a chat when we used to go on holidays to Haputale or Hatton, and Uncle Cliffy showed us round his wonderful garden and Auntie Eileen of course was always turning out some yummy eats! When Uncle Cliffy passed away Auntie Eileen was totally heartbroken. Gradually her health diminished and after some years she too left us.

Later on, Mrs Weeraratne built an additional large flat in front of the one we occupied, for her daughter Evan and her children. Evan had two daughters and two sons. The elder daughter Nilanthi was around seven years old and the second daughter Sharmini was around five; sons Gihan were about three and Rohan was a baby. Sharmini used to pop in at our place almost daily and listen to stories and play games with us! My dad had told her that she had to greet everyone whenever she came into our house and say 'bye' when she left – so this was a case of a rushed 'Hello hello hello and 'Bye 'bye 'bye', that took place so many times a day! We did love having them around! My dad as usual chatted to the 'smallies' and they loved coming home to play games and also to have the little bites my mum regularly turned out!

I recall the time Auntie Eileen invited us to her birthday party and had asked Sharmini as well. She was thoroughly excited and when my dad told her he would give her a present to take for Auntie Eileen, she was even more excited! They sat out in the garden and were busy packing a box with the gift inside, while I was doing my homework at the dining table and mummy was cooking as usual. After a while Sharmini smilingly left the gift with us and rushed home to get ready for the party.

We all asked the same question from my dad. "What was that you were packing for such a long time?"

"Well – er – it's a surprise so I don't want to spoil it for her!"

All dressed and ready to go, Sharmini rushed to our place looking like a little fairy! Grabbed the present now tied with coloured bows and a birthday card as well! Better looking than our gifts!! Hmm.

We walked up the stairs with Sharmini first in line. Auntie Eileen was standing right there and Sharmini gave her a hug and kiss and said, "Happy Birthday Auntie" and with shining eyes held the gift in both hands and presented it to Auntie Eileen. We followed wishing and giving and then joined the crowd to mingle, eat and chat!

The next morning Auntie Eileen came down to have a chat with us. She smiled, "I wanted to thank all of you for your lovely presents – so kind of you! But there was one thing I was puzzled about."

"Puzzled?" my mother said.

My dad said he had to go out for a meeting and jumped into the car and left the house.

I stood with ears hooked and eyes glued.

Auntie Eileen turned her head, "I brought it for you to see." She put a box with a whole pile of newspapers and coloured wrapping and ribbons and a card on the table. "What's this?" my mum said.

"It is the wrapping for the gift that Sharmini gave me."

'Oh dad's,' I thought, my heart beating fast.

Auntie Eileen lifted out a set of brass door hinges. "This was the gift." She looked up at mummy whose face was full of frowns.

"Er – excuse me – I have some homework to get done – talk to you later Auntie," smilingly I walked into the bedroom and shut the door. I had my ear glued to the door.

"That's really weird, isn't it?" Auntie Eileen.

"Yes – she's a small girl and doesn't understand about gifts…"

Auntie Eileen laughed, "Oh yes I know – I'm not angry or anything – but just curious as to who wrapped this up so beautifully – perfectly – except for the newspapers and the hinges." She laughed again.

My mum's voice came through. "OK Eileen, let's sit on the verandah and have a ginger beer and a chat!" And so, they chatted and sipped their drinks.

Gihan loved playing with water! Whenever he saw me watering our plants he would come to 'help' – which I didn't much appreciate as I loved doing this by myself – (still love watering plants!) – so I had to do it secretly but somehow, he would hear the gush of water and come running out of their house! I knew he had an 'afternoon nap' till about 4 o'clock so I had to do my plant watering before that! Bit of a problem – as I used to get back from school around 2 pm and then wanted to take a short nap myself – apart from the homework and other school work I had to do! My dad helped out! He used to get back at about 5.30 and he would take Gihan around watering their plants that faced our house. They did this with a watering can – and yes it was to pour a bit on the plants and a bit on his feet – so he loved doing this with my dad! Once they were all dressed up to go out and waiting for his grandmother to get ready when Gihan came over looking very smart and did the watering himself. The little watering can was left by our house so he picked it up, filled it with water and did the 'one for the pot, one for my feet' routine – when his mother discovered him all soaked with water she wasn't happy at all and dashed with him into the house to change his outfit! After that he wasn't allowed to come near our house in the evenings! My sister Lorni had now started her Secretarial classes so when she got back she would always look forward to my dad's surprises too! She made friends with the Weeraratne's and especially Marie who was a daughter of the landlady Mrs Weeraratne.

Every evening I would wait for the surprises my dad brought home! One day he brought a cushion which made a strange growly 'preeaww' sound when you sat on it. I kept sitting on it and we were both screaming and laughing at the weird noise it made. My mum of course didn't know anything about this as she was talking to the little kids in the garden. Some of our cousins and aunts and uncles were coming over to dinner and this was the opportunity! Lorni was very close to all my cousins so she joined in all the chatter and laughter that went on. During this babble I quietly slid the cushion onto an empty chair – while serving the patties of course! My uncle sat down and 'preeeaw' – he turned around on the seat and again 'preeaw' my dad continued to talk to him and the noise of the chatter was becoming louder. My uncle got up and walked towards the bathroom. My aunt was the next. Always beautifully clad, she sat gently and crossed her legs – her skirt edging her knees and her feet shod in shoes with slim long heels pointed to the floor. She moved and 'preeaw'; frown on her face, shift and again 'preeaw' "Gosh – what's that?" with the next 'preeaw' she stood up and with a puckered brow she too ambled towards the bathroom. My cousins were next – dinner was served and everyone was moving towards the table. I ran out and moved the cushion to another chair. My cousin sat with a plonk and 'preeaw' – "Oh God what the hell is that!"

"Hey you did something rude! – you did a – you know what!" his sister shouted. Laughter and giggling filled the room.

"You come and sit here and see." She sat and 'preeaw' – then they knew lifting the cushion they pressed it and heard its scream again! "Hey it's this damn cushion! From where the hell did you get this?" All eyes pointed at me.

I just shrugged my shoulders, 'Got a present.'

Laughs again!

My mum came in to check on us – did we have enough to eat? Did we need some water to drink? The chaos was on when she walked in and then she heard the 'preeaw' sound and looked quite startled. "What on earth is that?"

"Nothing nothing nothing – just a – a…"

She glared at me. 'A what?' she snapped.

"No – he just has a bit of a bad stomach – you know – that sound…" These were unmentionable words to her. She went over to my cousin who was seated on the chair and lifted him up like an invalid and walked him towards the bathroom. My cousin wore a grim face. As they left we put our hands to our mouths and choked on silent giggles. My sister who was seated with us sensed the danger of the scene and went into the kitchen to serve some short eats for us. My task was of course to rescue the cushion – I knew that would be next in line for my mother!

Quick grab and cushion in hand I dashed to my room and placed it under my pillow. Hopefully safe! Remember not to sleep on it!

After the guests left my mum and I were getting the place back to order. She was on the verandah picking cushions from each chair turning them this way and that, pressing hard on them. No sound whatsoever. I kept my eyes on the glasses and empty plates and collected them for washing up. I gave a side glance at the cushion examiner. No luck for her!

"Wonder what could have happened to that cushion?" She stared at me.

I shrugged my shoulders. "Goodness knows – maybe someone took it away. I mean it was a fun thing what!"

"Call that fun?" she stormed out of the room.

There was a clerk who had retired from dad's office who kept constantly visiting us to get my dad to try to get him some reemployment. Despite the pension and other gratuities he received, he would insist on getting some kind of work in the office. Every day when my dad got home after work, this clerk would be standing by the gate waiting to meet him!

I went in quickly and arranged the chairs – saw that the cushions were placed well where my dad was to meet him. Dad greeted him with a smile and asked him to come in.

"So, what can I do for you?"

The clerk handed over some documents.

"That's the thing Sir – I want an extra job because I don't like to just stay at home. I have enough money and all that but I like to be in the office. I will even pay you something to get in."

My dad's eyes glowered. He crumpled his lips and cleared his throat. "No no, I don't want any money – sit down and let's just discuss it."

The clerk sat on the chair and as he made himself comfortable a 'preeaww' sound emanated from his bottom.

Dad looked up, "What was that?"

The clerk shifted his bottom on the chair and once again 'preeaww' in a high pitch broke out.

Just then my mother who was just walking into the house gasped. "Oh my – is something wrong with you?"

"No Madam – it's just that – he shifted again and a very loud 'preeaww' came out. He jumped up and put his hand behind his back.

Mum's eyes turned green. "Come inside and have a cup of tea – that should do you good." She held his arm and guided him to our little dining table.

She walked back fast and grabbed the cushion before

we could do anything. Then armed with the cushion she went into the kitchen to make the tea. The cushion was chucked into the bin.

The clerk sat down gingerly waiting for the tea.

I went into the kitchen and a hand grabbed my shoulder. "Get out of the kitchen - don't touch the bin!" I dashed out.

She sat next to the clerk at the table. "Here have your tea – milk and sugar?"

He nodded and began to sip the tea.

"Do come again – I'm sure my husband will help you."

The clerk smiled and nodded. My dad worked up a smile and nodded in return.

"I'll go now – I'll bring all the papers you will need Sir. Thank you Sir, thank you Madam." He left. We watched him walking out of the gate.

My mum rushed to the back garden and tore the cushion 'preeaww' sounds again emanating from it and then plonked it back into the garbage bin. Silence.

She glared at my dad – "You are not to bring any of that nonsense stuff again." Then she turned to me. "Go – wash the clothes in the basin – and put them on the line."

Next evening the clerk was at the gate again. I went to the gate and spoke to him. My mum followed me – what next? Just then my dad turned his car into our premises. He stopped at the gate and spoke to the clerk, and handed him an envelope. The clerk smiled and put his hands together. Mum had been grabbing my arm all the while. Once inside she spoke to my dad. "What was all that about?"

"Got him a temporary job in one of the offices nearby – just to keep him going."

Mum's eyes softened and so did mine.

It was while we were at de Fonseka Road that my mother discovered a friend of hers living down Layards Road – which was just around the corner from us. We visited Aunty Lena Crozier and found that she worked in the Methodist Church Office which was next to my school. Aunty Lena's niece Dawne who lived with her was also just starting school at Methodist College and my mum once again took charge and arranged for Dawne to go with me to school! At that time my dad was working as an Administrative Officer in the Health Ministry in Colombo which was located at the former Parliament building at Galle Face, so he used to drop me off at school on the way to work. My mum gave me a task every morning – I had to walk to Layard's Road, get Dawne and walk back with her to our place and then jump into the car! Dawne and her aunt lived in a lovely spacious house which had an enormous garden. Dawne and I became good friends and I loved going to her place to spend the day. The large area at the back was where Dawne's grandfather used to breed bees! Her grandfather used to always take us to his bee garden where we had to wear protective nets over our heads and body and help him collect the honey! Ooh what a time with those bees buzzing right on our heads!! Dawne's father Shelley Crozier lived out of Colombo. He was a jungle lover and an ornithologist and is associated with the story of the Devil Bird which is a well-known legendary tale in Sri Lanka. Both Dr R. L. Spittel and Sir Christopher Ondaatje refer to him in their books. I also recall Uncle Shelley visiting the house at Layards Road and loved to listen to his jungle stories!

However, after some months this ground floor flat also proved to be too cramped a place for us so once again we moved – this time to a lovely large house at Milagiriya Avenue – located off the Galle Road – on the seaside opposite Dickman's Road.

1957 – 18 MILAGIRIYA AVENUE

I was now a teenager and looked forward to moving to this spacious house! Our friends Barney and Albert La Brooy owned this house and they wanted to rent out the larger side of it as they felt they could manage with a smaller area. The garden wasn't sprawling but large enough for us to have a billing tree, a karapincha tree and many flowering plants – so it was quite pleasant. Barney and Albert had a cute son called Philip who was about three or four years old at the time. We grew to be very close friends and enjoyed being in the same compound. Barney was an excellent dressmaker and was always busy with her sewing. Philip spent lots of time in our house and we loved having him over. Our neighbours on one side were the Jansz family – yes, the same name as ours but not relatives! Lionel and Phyllis Jansz had three sons Bevil, Travis and Derek. Aunty Phyllis was a professional dressmaker too. Right in front of our house was an empty plot of land and uncle Lionel had his little chicken farm there and I loved looking at them! On the other side we had the Perera family and their daughter Edith also became a very close friend of our family. There were the Thiagalingams, Sunderalingams, Jayalingams, and Nirmalingam – the Flamer-Calderas and also Nimal Mendis living down this road. The best thing was that the Chinese Dragon Café was at the top of the road and it was our favourite place for a snack of lime juice and potato chips! The other wonderful thing was that we could walk down the road to the beach and enjoy the view of the sea.

Once again, weekends were fun times. I used to walk down to the beach and walk back – my exercise for the day ☺.

We noticed a man who used to walk along the road picking up stuff from the sides particularly from a drain which ran on one side. He never made eye contact with us and would just rush past peering downwards. He would discard the remnants of his gatherings all over the road – pieces of paper, an envelope, a ribbon! We thought maybe he was searching for food so my dad suggested we put some toffees and biscuits in a small bag and place them on the side of the road. Peeping through the window I saw him pick them up then open the bag and fling it into the drain on the side! What?

My six toffees, gone! We went outside – there they were toffees and biscuit pieces all covered in mud and slime!

A few days later when I was walking up the road I saw him carrying a large brown envelope. He held it under his arm then took it out and looked at it while walking. A bit later I saw him walking past again with the envelope closely pressed against his chest. Went outside with shears to trim the flowering creepers which overhung our wall. Then I saw him dig into his pocket and pull out a cigarette. Puffing away, he sat on the edge of the drain and leaned against the boundary wall of the house that stood by it. He stretched out his legs, kicked off his slippers – then opened the envelope. He took out papers – first one, then another, then another, then, 'Aaaahhhh' a scream and something flew out and landed on the edge of the road. He ran down the road shouting and cursing! I just had to see what this was all about! By the edge of the road was the large envelope – with a dead rat on top of it! Oh gosh! Needless to say, this man was never seen down our road after this!

My mum continued with her expert cooking and seeing to all the household matters. We knew that the food would be served on time – breakfast, lunch, tiffin and dinner and everything would be in perfect order. My mum also trained me to clean up my room, and had me arrange my bed perfectly before I left for school. The sheets had to be arranged straight and neat, the pillows on the correct level and finally the 'bed spread' placed over with ultimate neatness! Whenever I got back home after school my mum would give me a cup of her yummy iced coffee and I would sit on my chair on the verandah to 'rest' after my hectic day at school! I well recall how on some days when I entered our house after school, my mum would ask me "How's your bed?" I couldn't understand what this was – how's my bed?

"Why what's wrong with my bed?"

"Take a look." She walked away.

I would go to my bed and – oh gosh I had not tidied it before I left for school! She had pulled down the bed spread and there it was – the sheet all crumpled and yes one pillow was under the bed. Oops! So, I had to tidy it up perfectly before I had the chance of having my iced coffee!

My mum also decided that I should learn how to cook! So, I had to help her in all her culinary activities! I learned to make sandwiches, iced coffee – which I loved and used to scrape all the condensed milk and gulp it down. Love cake – also had a lot of yummy ingredients which I yanked off the mixing bowl! Then came the Lamprais – a typical Dutch recipe which had a lot of preparation involved – we got the plantain leaves from our neighbour and these had to be cut and warmed and made ready! Then the food itself which took the entire day to make. Then serving it on the leaves and wrapping it up neatly. My mum was very particular that it should be just 'one bowl of rice'. So, my job was to fill this little bowl which she gave me and turn it over on the banana leaf neatly and she would fill in the rest.

Of course, this would go on for hours too – so to cut the time limit I would add more rice and plan for less packets! But – yes, she did spot this and gave me a good telling off – so I had to abide by the rules!!

My dad delighted in making us cups of Milo every morning – so he too was busy before he left for the office!

CHRISTMAS TIME!
Preparations for Christmas began with the lists! First there were the cards – all hand written and posted to friends and relatives. Then the list of presents – my dad and I loved to do all this, so gifts were selected carefully for each person and secretly wrapped in special paper! I know my mum and sister did the same in choosing gifts for my dad and me. What they didn't know was that my dad would always disclose my present to me and ask me not to tell anyone about it! There was this case of the Brownie Box camera that I'd seen in the Cargills Christmas catalogue. My parents had decided that this was to be for me. In the evening when my mum had gone in for her shower my dad and I quickly went through our list. Yes, he had bought some of the stuff and I had to hide it in my almirah – those large wooden cupboards made out of Burma teak and bought from Don Carolis. The presents were stuffed right at the back of the shelf behind all the folded blouses and skirts. Nobody would find them there. Then he looked furtively around and whispered, "You're getting a camera." His eyes gleamed. My eyes gleamed. "Don't

tell anyone," he continued, "Don't tell mummy whatever happens." I swore not to ☺.

Mummy was busy buying the ingredients for the many tasty goodies she made for Christmas. Long lists and long shopping hours and finally we unloaded the gigantic bags from our car!

First, we prepared the large rectangular baking pans which had to be lined with several layers of brown paper all buttered and moist to prevent any part of the cake sticking to the bottom and sides.

Then the action began! Each cake she made required different ingredients ranging from pumpkin preserve, ginger preserve, candied peel, raisins, sultanas, cherries and the list went on and on! So, from one day to the next, ingredients were selected for the special cake she'd be making and chopped by hand, then there would be flour, semolina, butter, sugar and eggs, and the various essences – vanilla, rose, almond and spices such as cinnamon, nutmeg and clove. These would be mixed again by hand in our special yellow bowl kept for this day!! Next, the oven would be lit and set to the correct temperature and the baking pans carefully lowered onto the racks. Then all we had to do was wait and wait and wait – a good two and a half hours sometimes! The pile of washing was mountain high but I was inevitably there to take over this task – the attraction being that I would rub my finger into the mixing bowl which always had a layer of cake mix – and tasted absolutely divine!

The evening brought the baked cake to the table and we each would have a taste of it licking our fingers after each piece! But mummy knows this 'tasting' would never end and quickly takes it away.

In a couple of days my mum has done the Christmas cake, Christmas Pudding, Love Cake, Breudher, Mince pies and also some homemade ham and roast chicken which are kept in our little deep freeze to be taken out for the special day!

Shopping for Christmas gifts was a real treat. We would go to shops in the Fort, Pettah and Maradana – some of the names I recall were Cargills, Apothecaries, Millers, Caves, Whiteaways, K. V. G. de Silva's bookshop, Carwallios and Titus Stores. In Pettah or Maradana the pavements were jam-packed with stalls selling crackers, decorations, Christmas cards, clothes, bags and hundreds of other interesting trinkets!

Buying the Christmas tree is a task my dad and I undertook. We would drive along the roads at Maradana where trees would be stacked leaning against the short parapet walls of the houses and other buildings. The tree sellers kept shouting the prices of their trees and sometimes became quite aggressive in their sales pitch! They opened up the trees to show us how large the branches were and how tall the tree was and how wonderful it was going to look in our house! After going through about a dozen or more trees we would decide on the one we want. We would hire a small van to carry the tree back to our place. Once home, we would unpack it very carefully so that the branches don't break!

Now we are all ready to set up the tree! We get a bucket, place the tree trunk in it, and fill it with sand topped with pieces of brick to steady it. Then we cover this with green crepe paper and arrange a red mat of crepe paper around the bucket and then start decorating the tree. The box of decorations and lights lay nearby and my sister Lorni and I would begin to decorate the tree. The final star on top was of course done by dad, who would stand right at the top of the ladder and fix it. I would run the paper garlands of silver and gold around the tree and my dad would do the same with the tiny lights that blink on and off and gave it a magical spark!

The Nativity Crib was also a major part of the décor in the house. I would stand on the ladder and retrieve the cardboard box from the top of a cupboard in the store room. Opened, it would reveal the tiny figures of Mary and Joseph, a crib with the Blessed Baby Jesus, shepherds, and angels which are hung with invisible thread. There are animals too – lambs, sheep, cattle and even a dog. I first put some straw and then arrange it so it looks very special placed on a table against the wall of the sitting room. Gold stars would be pasted on the wall to complete the picture.

My dad would be in charge of decorating the house. Here too I would be his assistant! The Christmas tree was placed in a corner of the living room. The box of decorations unpacked from its hidden shelf of the store room. We would unravel the long coloured streamers of paper and I would carry the small step ladder into the verandah. My dad would then climb right to the top of it and I would hand him one end of a strip which he fixed onto a nail already placed in a high nook just under the ceiling. He would twist it several times so that the straight piece of paper is now transformed into a series of waves which move delicately from side to side and swing with more force when I put on the overhead fan. We would have to decide what colour goes where and whether they match and, in a few hours, we have strung enough strips to make it look like a carnival!

The night before Christmas we are all excited about arranging the gifts at the bottom of the tree. I see the box camera I am to receive all wrapped up in a bright red paper with bells and mistletoe printed on it. My mum looks at me and smiles – what a lovely surprise for me she thinks! My dad looks away and I keep my eyes away from them. I am practising the surprised look I will have to wear when it's given to me! We have our dinner and I can barely sleep as I think of that camera! I can't wait to hold it and think of the number of pictures I will take with it! The night is quiet and even our dog and cat are fast asleep. Only I seem to be awake!

Christmas morning! I am the first to wake up. I run to the tree and gaze at the gifts under the tree. But I know I must not open them until the whole family is awake and gather together to open our presents! Everyone gets up early. We have our showers, gulp down a quick cup of tea, eat some fruit and get ready to go to church! We dress quickly in our special Christmas clothes. The church is full and we listen with intent to the story of the birth of Christ and the three kings who visited him and the angels who welcomed him with songs of praise. The story of Mary and Joseph and the special child who was born in a humble stable still had the magic of hope and blessing for us all. We knew most of the carols by heart and sang them with great joy. Music rings through the church and we herald yet another Christmas day!

When we get back home it's time to share the gifts! My dad and mum hand out their gifts to us. My sister gives us gifts too and I in my own small way hand out my tiny handmade treasures to my family. Touching the wrapped up camera gives me a thrill. I keep it for the last. My sister has given me a lovely bag to take to my ballet class and also a book of Animals of the World – something I have been eyeing in the bookshops these past few weeks! She loves the box I have made for her and the beautiful handbag my parents have given her. Daddy is raving over his shirt and tie and mummy delights in her perfume – and the beige handbag with the gold coloured clip. "Oh, these are perfect!" she says!

The floor and chairs are a mass of wrapping paper and cards and everyone is in good spirits. Only one gift remains unwrapped. I take it from the chair where it has lain all these precious minutes.

"Oh, what's this?" I say aloud and shake the box. Mummy is smiling and daddy looks nervous – will I play my part well? My sister looks unperturbed – she doesn't know about this☺. The camera in its black shiny case is wonderful to see and I say so with such genuine feeling that even I am surprised at myself.

"Do you like it?" Mummy asks.

"Like it? I *love* it!" I say holding to my chest. "It's great. Now I can take all the pictures I want!"

We sit down for breakfast and mummy places the breudher she has made – a Dutch recipe for a sweet type of bread – with the butter and Edam cheese we eat with it. It's so delicious that we can't stop eating! Another slice and another slice and … yes just one more slice!

The Christmas records are set in the radiogram – which is a combination of a radio and a record player – which my dad had got for us. It had a ten-record player so that when one record finishes playing it moves on to a side and the next one just falls on the platter and automatically plays – something quite innovative at that time! So, we hear Christmas songs and carols all day through! Lunch is a simple meal after which we clear up and then take a nap. Then we have to get ready for the grand meal of the day which is dinner!

First the table is arranged. Dishes are pulled out, napkins folded, placemats and plates set in place, glassware and cutlery all arranged. Bon-bons are placed on all the tables around the sitting room and verandah and also by the side of each plate so that the guest could pull them after dinner. Bon-bons are those little cylindrical paper holders containing a minuscule cracker and a small toy. Two persons pull at both ends and the cracker gives a short burst of noise and the toy is released from inside. I shake the bon-bons trying to guess what could be inside. Perhaps a fancy chain or a pencil cutter or a paper puzzle?

Guests arrive – friends, cousins, aunts and uncles – there is much noise in the greetings and after being served my mum's special treats – Christmas cake wrapped in red and green cellophane paper, love cake cut into bite size pieces, bowls of walnuts with a nutcracker which makes it great fun to use, mince pies and chicken pastry puffs. The adults drink the milk wine and we, the youngsters, drink Lanka Lime, Portello, Orange Crush and mum's special iced coffee!

Then we hear the carol singers – groups of youngsters and some elders too – from our Church and other Churches as well who come around and sing carols just outside our gate. We join them in some of the singing and serve them some cake and soft drinks and a cash donation for the community activities they are involved in.

Dinner is served! The table is laden with large platters – pieces of roast chicken, slices of homemade ham, sauces to go with these, bowls of salad, boiled vegetables and round bread rolls and butter cut into little pieces served in a glass bowl.

After the main meal we await the dessert which is a specially made Christmas pudding. The lights are turned off and, in the kitchen, I carefully pour a few spoons of brandy in the hollowed out top of the pudding. My dad strikes a match and the blue flames that surround the pudding are greeted with shouts of praise as I carry it into the dining room on a silver tray. The butter mixed with icing sugar stands next to it in a crystal bowl.

Everyone eats and talks at the same time so there is a constant buzz in the room. The records play popular carols – *Silent Night, O Come All Ye Faithful, O Holy Night*, and finally *Jingle Bells* where we all join in the singing!!! The lights on the tree twinkle off and on. The streamers on the verandah are swinging with great gusto. We feel the presence of our Lord Jesus Christ, which brings a feeling of love and joy among those gathered in our house on that special day.

After everyone leaves we have mounds of dishes to wash up. My sister, mum and I clear the table and take the dishes to the kitchen where Leela, our maid whose home was in Maskeliya and who had been with us for over five years, will wash them and put them to dry on the large centre table. My dad locks the doors, shuts the windows, sees that our doggie Kim is safely inside, switches off the lights and turns off the record player. By the time we get to bed it is way past midnight. As I creep into my bed I am too sleepy and tired to think of anything but snuggling into my soft pillows. My last thoughts are of the camera I now own☺.

BACK TO OUR NORMAL ROUTINE
Our house was slowly filling up with my parents, my sister (who was in her twenties and I was around thirteen) myself and then there was a spare room in front where a family friend stayed with us for a while. When she left, a friend of Lorni's from work – Katy

Benjamin moved in – she also stayed for a short time. When she left and the room was empty, it was not long before we had a friend asking us whether we could have another friend over! We asked her who this person was – Kamala Fernando, she said – she was from Kandy and had just passed out from Peradeniya (English Honours) and was teaching at Visakha Vidyalaya which was not too far from where we lived. So, one evening Kamala came over with her brother Anton – who was a doctor, and her fiancé Frank Samaraweera to meet us. While chatting my dad realised that Kamala's father was a close friend of his while we lived in Kandy. Without batting an eyelid, he said, "Of course she can stay with us – her father and I were close friends, and his daughter is always welcome to stay with us." So, the next thing we knew was that Kamala came over with her bags and moved into our front room! Kamala helped me with my English school assignments – I learnt so much about English literature – prose, poetry and drama – and enjoyed my work in school! Kamala would become one of my dearest friends.

One afternoon while roaming around the Kollupitiya market we met a cousin of my mother's and she told us that they lived out of Colombo and her daughter who was working in Colombo was looking for a place to stay. Before you could blink your eyes, my mother had told her to tell her daughter to bring all her stuff and come home the next day! So, she came! And this was Chi-Chi who also became my wonderful friend. Now we had my sister, myself and 'second cousin' Chi-Chi in the room my sister and I shared. Of course, when Chi-Chi moved in my sister insisted on keeping 'her half' of the room and so I had no choice but to share 'my half' with Chi-Chi! In addition, we had Kamala in the front room. And my parents of course who had their own room! We were a family of animal lovers so we had one doggie – a Cocker-Spaniel called Kim, two cats, and many birds and squirrels who took over our garden as their playground! So, to say that our house was jam-packed was an understatement!

Chi-Chi who was not only a very attractive girl was also quite a madcap, and ever ready to have a fun time – so together we planned and plotted and went through our adventures! I well recall the Chinaman – as we used to call him who came around on his bicycle laden with materials of all sorts, ranging from cottons to silks to flimsy nylons. He used to lay them out on a paper on the verandah and we had to choose. I would be so dazzled with all the colours, designs and textures that I would want everything! My mother of course did the selecting and chose fabrics out of which she would sew dresses and other garments for herself, my sister and me. Readymade clothes were unheard of and one had to either sew them oneself or get them tailored. Then the cries of the *thrombol* man who brought all kinds of everything – from golden coloured bangles, buttons, braid and lace edging of all shades, sewing thread and a multitude of knick-knacks. Once again, I was totally engrossed in looking at everything that I felt I could take all his boxes of treasures, and yet again my mother tolerated no nonsense from me and only purchased what was really necessary! But if I pleaded with a sad look in my eye she would buy me a fancy brooch or a set of hair slides! Chi-Chi of course would smother these salesmen with her charismatic smile and would buy something at a lesser price!!

Then there was the kadalai man who used to go past pushing his cart full of an incredible selection of gram, shouting 'Kadalai' at the top of his voice. I used to dash out of the house with Chi-Chi and we used to take ages to pick and choose, to see which was better and which would give us a bigger *gotta* (a paper cone which held the gram). Chi-Chi would blink and I am certain even wink at the kadalai man and we would end up getting an extra *gotta* from him! There was also the godamba roti man who would scream out his wares "Godambaa godambaaaa" and this too would take us out to buy his delicious godamba roti which he deftly made then and there flattening the little balls of dough and swishing them from side to side to get the most delicate godamba ever! Here too, my pretty second cousin would cast her magic eye on him and we would always get a couple of extra godambas plus sambal! My mother just believed that these men were 'good' men (which no doubt they were) and were giving these extras as a goodwill gesture, until one day she too came to the carts with us and was simply horrified at the behaviour of my cousin. Mummy gave us one of her green-eyed stares which sent us in scuttling and ever since then she always accompanied us when the godamba and kadalai sellers turned up!

Now we were thrown out from two of our ventures – we had to think of something new! We often had visitors – yes handsome young guys – to see my sister I'm sure! I would keep a lookout to ensure that my mother wasn't around (she was usually having a shower or in the kitchen at this time). Then Chi-Chi would appear on the verandah dressed in a fancy cloth and jacket with a broom in her hand. She would come near the boys who were seated on the verandah and smile at them and say in a very soft voice "Aney Sir, kakul podak aiyn karanda puluwanda?" (Can you please move your feet a little?) My sister would be too stunned to say anything and I was standing by the window trying hard not to burst into laughter!! The boys would gaze at her and then slowly move and maybe even get up from their seats while she swept under the chairs and moved onto the inside of the house. Of course, I would tell her to quickly go in and change before my mum came out. I'd collect the dust and fling it into the dustbin. The bathroom door opened and my mum came out and went into her room. She must have been happy to see me actually doing some work! Meanwhile Chi-Chi was doing a quick change of clothes in our room! And of course, when they next visited, the boys asked my mother where that lovely girl who used to sweep the place was. My mother then knew who the scoundrel was! That was it – another venture down the drain!

Now we had to think of something else. But what?

As usual Chi-Chi came up with a brilliant idea. We had a very handsome young man who used to visit us

– once again a friend of Lorni's! But he became quite friendly with our family and often had dinner with us. So, we became firm friends. One day while my sister was in the shower, Chi-Chi and I sat out and chatted with him. Then Chi-Chi said she wanted to go and rest as she had a headache and excused herself from our group. A short while later a girl came out wearing a long skirt and blouse and with her hair in a single plait and smiled shyly at Mr Handsome ☺. I looked up – kept silent. She said, "Hello I'm Chi-Chi's twin sister Sherine."

He gazed up at her and continued to do so when she very silently pulled a chair forward and sat nearby. He just kept gazing. Speechless. Head in a whirl.

"So – how come I haven't seen you here before?"

"I live with my parents at Udawattakella – hardly ever come down to Colombo." She smiled. Her voice soft and gentle.

"Do you work anywhere?"

"No – I just work at home, helping my mum and I do some sewing." She looked down and adjusted a pleat on her skirt. She stood up. "Sorry you must excuse me – I have some packing to do, as we leave in a little while."

"What do you mean? You're going back?"

I was just outside in front of the verandah, watering the plants and could hear this conversation clearly. I heard my mother calling me from the kitchen so I immediately stopped and dashed back to the kitchen unnoticed by the two having their chat!

"Yes. So, Cheerio!"

"Cheerio – I hope I'll see you the next time you come. When will you be coming next?"

"I'm not sure at all – when my parents decide to come, then I will come."

Then Chi-Chi was in the room – changing her clothes. I was chatting to my mum.

I came out and my sister was chatting to Mr Handsome. Phew – that was close!

Chi-Chi and I made a deal. I would keep watch while she was Sherine when Mr H. came next. Done!

There were several nexts – Mr H came but Sherine was still at her home. Once he came to the gate – "Is she here?"

"Coming next week – er – sometime" I replied.

So, the game went on – Sherine and I playing our roles!

Once when I got back after school I saw Barney in our house speaking to my mum.

They both looked confused. Now what?

My mum stopped me – "I never knew Chi-Chi had a twin sister – Sherine? Barney says her relative Mr H who comes here so often has fallen in love with Sherine and wants to contact her. Who is this person?"

I shrugged my shoulders, twisted my lips and shook my head. Ran to the bathroom. Oh Gosh what next?

I got on to the road with the doggie Kim – walk time. Could see Chi-Chi coming down after work. Met her

– "Hey you better get ready for an interrogation! Mr H has told Barney that he is in love with Sherine"

"What?" she looked down – "What the hell am I going to do?"

"Truth or hell."

That evening was a heavy discussion – mummy, my sister, myself and of course the twins turned into one. My dad of course was as usual at a work meeting and getting late!

The truth was revealed. Mummy spoke very harshly – "Do you know you have ruined that boy's entire life by your stupid jokes!" Glared at me "And you stupid creature thought this was funny ha? Both of you are personifications of evil! Go to his place and apologise – if you don't – you ChiChi can go to your home at Uda wherever – and you can stay in your room for the next month. I'm done with you!"

She walked away.

Chi-Chi and I sat silently – our minds in a whirl. Were we really wicked? Personifications of evil? Satan's children? — oh no no no —.

The very next day Chi-Chi and I went over to Mr Handsome's house in Colpetty. We knocked on the door. He opened and stared at her – eyes began to water.

She spoke, "I am really sorry for what happened – I came to apologise. Please forgive me – I shouldn't have done this – I was only playing the fool – didn't think you would take it so seriously."

I also looked in and spoke to him, "Really very sorry – we are all very fond of you and never meant to hurt you."

He just kept staring.

"It's okay." He spoke softly. "Really okay."

"Please come home again to see us – we miss having you visit."

"Okay – I'll come – sometime." He closed the door gently.

We returned home with relief.

Told my mother and she, Chi-Chi and I sat down and held hands.

After almost two weeks had passed with no signs of him we were all feeling very down. Chi-Chi and I mostly so. Then my mind zoomed! My parents – my sister! They were the ones who should speak to him – not us, after all we were the creators of the whole mess-up! So, my parents and my sister went to see him. He smiled when he saw them and asked them inside. They sat and had a chat. They didn't mention the chaotic incident. Two days later our doorbell rang. I peeped through the window, couldn't believe what I saw. He was there! I ran and told Chi-Chi and we peeped out of the bedroom door. Yes, there he was – smiling and my mum was hugging him and my sister was showing him a chair – they sat down and we could hear the chatter. Should we go out? No! I held us back. No – no no!

My mum came into our room and took us to the verandah. Chi-Chi and I stood together, heads down

– no eye contact. My mum took us towards him and he stretched out his hands to us. "All's forgotten now – let's be friends again."

Tears flowed down our faces. Sad and happy! Now we were friends again! That night we slept peacefully – all problems solved!

Our bathroom was at the end of a corridor and we all had a little torch in hand when we had to use it at night. One night while we were sleeping a figure peeped into our room and groaned 'Aurora', I heard it. Opened my eyes. Then again, 'Aurora' a deep growly voice – 'Aurora Aurora' – I jumped out of bed but couldn't find my torch. Chi-Chi leapt out of her bed, "Oh oh what was that – I'm sure it was a ghost – a ghost – oh my gosh."

I grabbed my torch from under my pillow and flashed it into the doorway – nothing.

Chi-Chi cried – "I'm not coming out – I'm not!"

"You stay – I'll check" I then saw a figure going into my parents' room. I hid behind the door and peeped inside. My dad was just creeping into his bed chuckling to himself. Then I knew.

"No one – no one – must have been a bad dream, right?" I said to Chi-Chi who was crouched on my bed when I spoke to her.

She said, "I can't sleep alone." Well, she took to

sleeping on my bed after this scary incident. She was on the wall side and I was on the outer edge. I nearly rolled off twice. Chi-Chi was sleeping soundly, breathing softly. Me? Catching on to the edge of the bed. No – this won't do! I got down and went across to her bed. Tucked myself in and soon fell asleep! Next morning, I woke up – and we both looked across at each other. She said, "What's happened? How are you in my bed – how am I in your bed?"

'Aurora!' I shouted.

"Oh my gosh yes – terrible – what was that?"

'Dad,' I said and laughed.

A few years later Chi-Chi's parents moved to Colombo and of course they wanted her to live with them. It was very sad to see her go. But I knew things had to change for all of us.

My memories of this fun loving wonderful person will always be with me!

Kamala also left us to go as she and her teacher friends had formed a group and found a set of quarters, they could use which was close to the school. So now it was just our family in the house!

My dad was always happy to drop me off at school. But I realised that sometimes when I wanted to go early it would be inconvenient for him to do this. So, I decided to use the bus, as the bus-stop was on the Galle Road close to our house. I soon got the hang of going in a bus and more often than not I would leave home at

7 am to get to school by 7.30. Some days I would leave really early – around 6 am when I wanted to play tennis with my friend Corinna Gauder before school began. Returning from school was easy as many of my friends took the bus back to their homes. So, this became my routine and I found it quite easy and convenient –and the double decker buses were really lovely! I would climb on to the top deck and peer down at the road while we travelled!

Often my school friends would come over to lunch or tea especially during the holidays. My friend Valerie Keyt who lived down Layards Road and I regularly visited each other. I used to walk up with her to the top of Milagiriya Avenue on the Galle Road – and she would cross over to Dickman's Road, turn around and wave to me, and then walk towards her house. Once when we were walking up she told me her family was planning to go to Australia. I thought it was for a holiday but when she told me that they were actually moving to Australia and didn't plan to return I was really shocked and felt very sad. I felt that I might never see this friend of mine again. I still remember seeing her walk away and do her usual turn around and wave to me and the tears filling my eyes. When I got back home and told this to my family they too felt sad that my dear friend was leaving us. Anyway, the wonderful thing is that we are still in contact with each other – after so many years!

Lorni and myself at the beach near Milagiriya Avenue.

Me at Milagiriya Avenue in my Methodist College uniform at the age of 12 or 13 years old.

Methodist College Class picnic when we were around fifteen years old.

Myself at Aunty Timmy's Dancing School

Myself holding my cat Blackie at the Milagiriya Avenue house.

Myself at the age of 21 or 22 years old when we lived down Charlemont Road.

Simon and myself after our wedding ceremony about to go on honeymoon, 1970.

SCHOOL DAYS IN COLOMBO – MEMORIES OF METHODIST COLLEGE

My first day at Methodist College sticks in my head! Pat Geddes very kindly accompanied me on my first day at school and introduced me to some of her classmates. They were very friendly and took me over to meet some of those who would be in my class (Pat was a year junior to me) so I didn't feel left out at all. There was I, a new entrant, standing on the playground of one of Colombo's most prestigious schools. I was in my new uniform but without a tie – a green tie – as it would be given to me once I was installed in a 'house' – I didn't know anything about the 'houses' but soon I would. My only friend Pat had to go to her own class so I was left with some other new girls awaiting my turn to get to my class.

It was Miss Dorothy Williams, the Chaplain of MC, who came over and took me by the hand and led me to my classroom. I can't remember the name of my class teacher but well recall that I was totally swept over with the number of new faces that met my eyes.

Anyway, the first day went off well with my name being announced and everyone looking back to check out the new girl in their class. I well recall some of the girls coming over and speaking to me – which I thought was so friendly and nice. I sat in the second row and had a desk of my own – like all the others did.

We had to gather in the school hall where Miss Grace Robins, our Principal at the time, (generally called 'Robs' by us!) welcomed the new girls and we had prayers and sang our school anthem *Praise my soul the King of Heaven* after which we went back to our classrooms.

A few days later we were summoned to a 'house' meeting and I discovered I had been allocated to Choate House – named after a former Principal of MC. The new girls were officially welcomed to a big round of clapping and cheering. We sang the 'house song' and then went back to class. So, there I was, securely embedded in my new school.

There were rules and rules! We had to stand perfectly quiet in line while going into the church for a morning service or to the hall for assembly. *Praise my Soul* and *I Vow to Thee my Country* are still some of my favourite hymns. The prefects were posted like security guards and if we so much as sneezed they would pull us out of line and give us a 'minus' mark – we would then have to go to the House Prefect and get a stern admonishment for 'misbehaving' and also for losing points for our House. A certain number of minus marks would send us to the Principal's office. We couldn't go out of the school premises during our lunch break without written permission either from our parents or school authorities. We couldn't eat lunch of rice and curry in the classroom but had to await our turn to eat in the hall which had tables and long benches set out for this purpose. At that stage of our lives, we decided there were too many rules hanging over our heads and were determined to see how many of them we could throw out of the window!

By the end of the First Term, I had made several good friends – some who stuck with me right to the end of my school career at MC and even to this day. We had by now formed groups to 'break the rules' and even the quiet, well behaved students in our class joined in all our pranks in their own quiet way of course! As we moved to higher classes we had new girls coming in as well as some girls leaving us. I was relieved to be promoted to the next Form the following year. By now my friendships had deepened and I had great fun with the 'naughty' girls in the class. Although I was quiet and not half as bold as they were, I was always ready to take 'instructions' and enjoy the 'results' of our outlandish actions! My leader was Corinna Gauder – who remained one of my closest friends – sadly she passed away a few years ago. My dear friend Mariam Mohamed also passed away a few years ago, as did Ripple Geddes who was Pat's cousin. Other friends were Aprille Aiyadurai, Sakina Galely, Barbara Bartholomeusz, Inaya Razee, Nobel Kiel, the two Valeries – de Soysa and Keyt, the two Gillians – Thorne and Smith, Grace Thomas, Jeanne David, Harisha Packirsaibo, Delrine Jonklaas, Deanna Clements, Maziya Sulaiman, Khaizaran Cader, Angela Deutrom, Meena Mangaram, Kamelesh Chand, Sundari Kundanmal, Koshu Sobraj, Warnesia and Dani Dole, Trudy Dickson, Dianne Ebert, Ann Medonza, Averil Lokubalasuriya, Cherrie Fernando, Priya Guruswamy, Shrini Attygalle, Shanti Samarasinghe,

Gene Edirisinghe, Jeanette Walpola, Juliet Meadows, Mano Candappa, Diana Peries, Gnei Razaak, Ruth Pinto-Jayawardena, Oreen de Alwis, Renee Samuel, Sharmini Armstrong, and Roshni Gunasekera who was also in Kurunegala with me! We had friends in the higher classes as well – so there was Sakina's cousin – who was also named Sakina Galely, and Evadne Aserappa. I still keep in touch with some of these friends! However – I am sure I've left out some names – which have escaped my wobbly memory– so those who are not included in this story please forgive me! We also had constant contact with those in the parallel classes – that is the Sinhala stream and the Tamil stream – and also with those in some of the higher classes. At that time, we had Burgher, Sinhala, Tamil, and Muslim girls who belonged to diverse religious and social backgrounds, but the differences didn't affect my friendship with them in the least. To me they were just wonderful people.

I am certain the teachers faced a real challenge dealing with us. The games period proved a challenge to me with Miss Cynthia Rasquinho being in charge! Netball was never my game but she insisted that I play and because of my short stature made me take the 'centre' position. Needless to say, I bungled up so much that after a couple of games she packed me off to play some other game!

The singing teacher gave up on us as she asked us to sing while she played the notes on the piano. All planned perfectly, we stood up and opened our mouths, wore animated expressions on our faces – and made no sound whatsoever! She must have thought she was going deaf after the second girl also did this. She kept saying that she couldn't hear anything – asking us (the class) whether we could hear and we seriously replied that yes of course we could hear –in other words (which we did not say) there was something wrong with HER! I'll never forget how she just slammed the piano shut and dashed off to Miss Robins to say that she could not and would not continue teaching our class! Needless to say, we were very sternly reprimanded by Miss Robins! Good news was that we were given a new teacher and we enjoyed our singing so much we never wanted the class to end!

We moved into a higher class and were allotted a new class teacher –this was Miss Shanthi Nonis who had just graduated and perhaps this was her first posting. Ah ha! We thought – a new young teacher – now's the time to start the fun! But did we get a chance? Not at all! She immediately changed our places – the girls at the back who were considered the naughty ones were brought in front and our seating was all reallocated – so the structure of the play was entirely changed, much to our dismay. She wrote something very diligently in a book while we were doing some written work. The next day we thought we could go back to our old seats – after all WHO would remember who sat where? But she did! She had written it all down – so we were absolutely foxed. Long after I had left school, Mrs Shanthi Peiris (nee Nonis) was appointed as Principal of Methodist College.

Then there was the very sweet Home Science teacher. We had no interest whatsoever in learning how to bathe babies or to make cakes at this time in our lives. Time to play – so we 'lost' the baby's head – thank goodness it was just a plastic doll! This caused quite a bit of chaos. A real drama arose when we had to make a cake and very stealthily added some chilli powder into the egg mixture to make it look brighter? Our teacher kept saying that the eggs looked rather dark in colour and my friend Barbie in all seriousness said that it was the 'reflection of her orange coloured saree!' Of course, the teacher tasted the mixture and was horrified at the burning sensation in her mouth! "Chilli powder" she screamed, "You have put chilli powder into the cake!" So once again we were sent to Miss Robins who must have been having serious nightmares at this time with us behaving the way we did!

I can never forget the drama when Nobel Kiel was selected Sportswoman of the Year – she was Ceylon's champion High Jumper. We were so thrilled to have our classmate in this grand position that we didn't hesitate to throw her up singing "She's a jolly good fellow" with great vim and vigour. Only thing was — we forgot to catch her once we threw her up – can you believe it! Yes, she landed on a desk or something and the next thing we knew was that an ambulance had to be summoned and she had to be rushed off to hospital. Mr Guy

Thiedeman – the official coach who trained our special athletes just screamed his head off at us – and yes once again off we went to Miss Robins!

The well-known artist Mrs Vinitha Fernando (nee de Silva) was, in my view, the most memorable art teacher. Until that time, we were used to doing regular pictures in regular paint box watercolours. Vinitha changed all that – we had a new Art room – set up where we gathered for our class. She passed around large sheets of paper and poster paints from little jars and various types of brushes. She told us that art was a 'subjective concept' and we could interpret our own perspective in our paintings. I was completely drawn into the world of art. She spoke to us about famous artists and the various techniques of art. To give us an example of still life she placed a basket of fruit on the table and told us to paint this as we saw it. Then she told us she would have to leave the class for a few moments to collect something from the office. We waited until she left the room, put someone on 'watch' and rushed to the fruits gobbling them up really fast! Then we placed the skins in the basket and on the table. When she entered the room, there we were, all in our seats and very seriously gazing at the 'still life' which had transformed into a chaotic bunch of fruit skins and seeds! She glanced at the mess and made no comment. We were thunderstruck. Shouldn't she have screamed at us? But she didn't. Hands went up one by one with questions such as "Miss – if the banana skins are there without the real banana, how do we paint this?" or "Miss the papaw has only the skins and the seeds are on the floor – so how do we paint that?" To which she calmly responded, "Art is what YOU see – so just go ahead and paint YOUR interpretation of what you see." That was the last time we ever tried our tricks on her!

There must be another thousand stories like this – but let me tell you something about the wonderful education I enjoyed at MC. Ms Rene Perera, Miss Siriwardena, Olga Drieberg, Irma de Motte, 'Mama' Mendis, Miss Williams, Mrs Muriel Aiyadurai, were some of the teachers I well recall. Mrs Marbit Gunasekera was our English Literature teacher and under her tutelage we enjoyed the classics – drama with Shakespeare, the prose of Jane Austen, Thomas Hardy, the Brontes, the poetry of Wordsworth, Tennyson and many others became a part of my life. I spent much time at the College Library and also joined the British Council Library which was located close to MC at the time. During the holidays I would visit the BC Library and read up all the books I wanted. However, we did discover that Marbit loved cats – so yes – any time we needed to distract the class all we had to do was to find a cat!

We had Eurythmics once a week and I got to know Timmy Ingleton – joined her school of dancing and did ballet and tap classes even after I had left school. I loved my dancing lessons and went to Aunty Timmy for many years enjoying the wonderful experiences of taking part in her concerts at the Lionel Wendt Theatre. Aunty Timmy remained a great favourite of mine.

The Sports Meet was a really big event for us. We practised for the 'march past' many times over and the athletes trained through their events all afternoon (once school was over)! On the day itself we had a Chief Guest and a great ceremony with raising of flags and singing the National Anthem and the College song. Everyone was hooked on getting their own house to win the games! So, there was plenty of shouting and cheering! We took part in singing and acting competitions and although I wasn't an actress I would assist in the backstage work in any play that was put on. We had fun times on class picnics and other outings.

After school our big treat was to go to Perera & Sons which was just opposite our school – a place which sold the most scrumptious cakes and 'short eats' as they called the patties, cutlets, and Chinese rolls. Usually about three or four of us would go. We would collect our money together – mostly ten, five and twenty-five cent coins and then decide what to buy to share among us! We selected with great care – was the patty in the third row slightly bigger than the others? The Chinese roll in the second row looked bigger than the others? It would take about half an hour to select – then to pay – counting, counting, counting all the coins – finally the full amount is reached – must have been about fifty-five cents for two patties, a cutlet and Chinese roll! Packet in our hands – now to share – who's going to take the first bite? Ah ha – that was too big – now see we are left with nothing! Almost an hour had gone – anyway we did have a bite – even though it was not as big as expected! Time to jump the bus and go home! So off to the bus-stand on the Galle Road and home we went – happy to have spent some good time together! I loved going on the red double decker buses. I used to climb up the little stairway in the bus and get to the upper deck, sit at the edges and peer down at the busy road. The fun thing we did here was to tear bits of paper and fling them out of the window then get back to our seats as we didn't want to be seen by those below! Once past them we would look out and see flakes of white fluttering down like snowflakes, with people looking up wondering what these were?

As a class we often interlinked with other classes and learnt how to form committees and plan small events, a wonderful experience to sharpen my organising skills!

Our curriculum comprised of arts and science subjects but when we got into Form 4 we had to make the choice of whether we were going to do Arts or Science for our O' Levels which would take place at the end of Form 5. I opted to do Arts and had to sit for eight subjects. After I had passed my O'levels I left school. I well recall my last day. I waited until my friends had gone home and then took a walk around the school and was swamped in sadness when I realised I would never sit at my desk again, never play badminton or tennis on these courts, never walk around the school rushing for classes. The time had come for me to leave so I just had to face it.

I didn't go to the University although many years later I did obtain a Diploma in English (Literature) through the External Programme conducted by the University of London. All the English grammar and literature I had learnt at MC came back to me at this point!

However, I did keep in touch with the school after I had left and was on the OGA committee for some years, when we had great fun organising carnivals for the public and having celebratory functions for the members. I recall Lylie Godridge who organised a choir from among the old girls and we had a concert – all dressed in green sarees and our event was even featured on a local TV programme at the time!

I am still in contact with many MCites. We recall all the old days and the fun times we enjoyed! To this day I have fond memories that make me not only smile but also laugh out loud! What I treasure most is the fact that we learnt to value people for what they were. This has been perhaps the most rewarding experience for me. My love for the arts – writing, reading, painting, music, dancing — my love for animals and nature, and my spiritual beliefs, were all boosted by my experiences at Methodist College.

Methodist College will always be there for me. May the school be blessed not only to reach the heights of academic and sporting goals but also in keeping with the MC motto *We Scatter Light* – spread the light of love and caring to all those around them. God Bless Methodist College!

Outside my school activities my passion was ballet and tap dancing. Timmy Ingleton, who had trained at the British Royal Academy of Dance in London and worked for Marjorie Sample (a well-known name in the field of dance at the time) subsequently opened her own Timmy Ingleton School of Dance. She was our Eurythmics teacher at school and when I heard she ran a private School of Dance I immediately joined! I remember her asking me why I wanted to learn ballet and I promptly replied, "I want to be Margot Fonteyn." "Hmm," she nodded. The next question was why I wanted to learn tap dancing. "I want to be Gene Kelley." She nodded again. Well, here was an about-to-be champion dancer – what? She smiled and told me I could come the following Saturday. The classes were held at her private residence located at Monsoon Lodge in Colpetty. She was married to Darley Ingleton and had two children Michael and Gillian. It was a spacious upstairs house with a large garden and was situated between the British Council (at that time) and the Colombo Swimming Club. Right from day one I felt quite at home in my dance class. Aunty Timmy, as she was fondly known by her pupils, always welcomed us with a bright smile. She was the epitome of neatness when it came to dress, always in a beautiful skirt and blouse, chain and earrings to match, and hair put up in a tidy bun. I was able to meet and later become friends with girls from different schools. In other words, not only did I learn to dance but also how to mix with children from diverse nationalities and backgrounds, for Aunty Timmy treated all of us alike. Aunty Timmy was the kindest teacher I've ever known. She would offer us iced drinking water from the bottles in her fridge and sometimes we used to take a smack of pudding as well!

In the class itself she took great care to see that each pupil understood what she demonstrated, and apart from the 'shoulders down, straight back, tummies in' instructions she would give us to start with, she would also walk around bending a hand here and repositioning a leg there. I never really saw her lose her temper. She was always swift to praise and slow to chide!

She used to have an annual concert with all the students participating. Rehearsals were at Ladies College and the concerts were held at the Lionel Wendt Theatre. These concerts were absolutely wonderful and I loved being on stage with a fantastic group of dancers – imagining I was Margot Fonteyn and Gene Kelly and revelling in the Strauss waltz sequences we performed! There were hardly any boys who did ballet at the time and I can only recall Michael (Aunty Timmy's son – who also later trained at the Royal Academy in London', and the Rankine brothers – David and Tony. Girls I remember were Anthea Peiries and Melanie Jansz, Kushlani (we called her Kushi – Ranasinghe), Virginia and Susan Swan, and Deirdre de Kretser. Here too some of the names are not very clear in my head so please excuse any blunders! As we needed another boy to complete our team for one of our Strauss waltz performances, Aunty Timmy asked me whether I could find someone suitable! So, I asked our close friend Michael Geddes (Pat's cousin) who had lived in England but came back for a few years. He was the first male hair stylist for women in the country and had his own salon where he used to live! Michael partnered me at the concert and when the cast discovered that he was also a hairdresser many of the girls would get him to style their hair before the performance – sometimes delaying his own presence on stage! So Aunty Timmy had to lay down some strict rules that did not permit anyone to get him to do their hairstyles backstage!

I well recall how once when one of the senior dancers fell ill and couldn't take part in the concert to be held that very evening, Aunty Timmy asked me whether I could do the part. I was flattered that she thought I was good enough, but also quite nervous at this last minute call! Knowing how worried I was, she took me aside and in her usual persuasive manner told me I would be just fine, and then she patiently showed me the steps which I practised over and over again with her in some obscure corner of the Wendt. Then I had to fit on the costume I was to wear and was in despair when it turned out to be far too big and long for me! This too she sorted out, and soon someone was busily taking up the hem and narrowing the sides. When the time came for the actual performance, she stood in the wings giving me all the encouragement I needed and I must say I came through the whole performance quite well – although my legs were like jelly when I left the stage! Another time I fractured my ankle during a dance class and she was absolutely distraught about this. She sent me a letter each week inquiring about my health, until I was well enough to visit her and show her that I was completely fit again! Even after I found employment in a mercantile firm at the age of twenty, I used to go after office hours to Aunty Timmy's for a workout. Unfortunately, other pressures compelled me to give up my dancing classes. Aunty Timmy migrated to Australia and sadly I lost touch with her. But I shall never forget my wonderful ballet and tap-dancing experiences with wonderful Aunty Timmy.

The British Council Library was located near Aunty Timmy's and was my other favourite place. I would spend a whole morning there rummaging through the books and trying to figure out which two I could borrow for the week! Once I got back home of course I buried myself in the books and was ready for my next read by the end of the week.

At Milagiriya Avenue, my cousin Allister Bartholomeusz and our family friend Gamini Seneviratne who was a senior journalist at the Times of Ceylon, visited us all the time. In fact, Gamini was at our place for almost all his meals! My sister and some of her friends used to join Allister, Kanaks, Turab, Aubrey – and his other swimming friends on their adventures at the Kinross Swimming Club at Wellawatte.

We were a family that also loved going to the movies and my parents would take me for almost all the change of films that moved around the Colombo cinemas – the Savoy, the Regal, the Majestic, the Olympia were the main cinemas. My school friends and I too would often get together and go to the movies – James Dean, Rock Hudson, Elvis Presley, Pat Boone, Frank Sinatra and Dean Martin were among the favourites! Bill Haley and the Comets came on the scene and brought in a new type of dance – the rock and roll – which we loved! My sister Lorni was an expert dancer and her jiving and rock and roll performances at our parties were simply fantastic!

I well recall how once at the Savoy there was a movie which featured Bill Haley and the Comets and when *Rock around the Clock* came on everyone began to clap and soon we were all rocking and rolling down the aisles of the cinema hall which sent the cinema attendants into a state of utter confusion! My friend Sakina and I saw *Giant* at least five times – she liked James Dean and I liked Rock Hudson! Sadly, James Dean died in a motor accident before the film was out and my friend really felt totally broken about this. She didn't come to school for almost a week! With my parents I would see more serious films. I'll never forget the time they made *Bridge on the River Kwai* in Sri Lanka. Director David Lean, and the actors Alec Guinness, William Holden, and Jack Hawkins were legendary names and we were thrilled when my cousin Allister Bartholomeusz who was a keen swimmer and his friends were involved in some of the underwater scenes in the film. The greatest thrill was that my good friend Pat's sister Christine Geddes actually had a speaking part in the film which made us see the movie at least five times! We would hold our breath, eyes stuck on the screen – there she was – and then the magic of her words came through!

Lorni was appointed to a Senior Secretarial position at Walker Sons where she worked until she wanted to have the chance of going abroad for a few years – just to experience living in a foreign country! Her friend Dawne at Walkers had gone to London some years before so this became Lorni's destination as well! She decided to visit England for a couple of years. We were sad to see her go but knew that she would be happy to meet up with Dawne and other friends in the UK. I'll never forget the day she left when we all dressed up to the core and went aboard the *Oriana* to say goodbye to her. There being no mobile phones or any other quick contact methods at the time, we had to wait for three weeks before we got a call from her from London to say that she had reached safely! We used to send her airmail letters – aerogrammes – every week and she would write to us too. Occasionally we would give her a call and that had to be planned with the greatest of precision. First, we had to inform the General Post Office that we wanted an overseas call to the UK and had to book this call – for a certain day at a certain time. Only then could we pick up the phone and speak to her, having only a few minutes before we were told that our time was up – sometimes the calls couldn't be received as there were heavy rains across the ocean near Britain so we just had to wait! Anyway, after two years we were very excited when Lorni mentioned that she had met a planter called William Bartholomeusz, who had gone to England on furlough – which was the practice with the foreign plantation companies in Ceylon at the time.

She said he was really nice ☺ and wanted him to meet us. He had returned home a few weeks back and we invited him over to have dinner with us. After all, we had to check out this guy who seemed to have won my sister's heart! So, the day arrived and we were all dressed up properly as my mum put it. I had to wear a dress and tie my hair neatly and wear proper shoes!! Well, he was due at 6.30 to meet and have a drink (only soft drinks remember). At 6.30 we heard a very noisy car charging up and down our road! Who the hell was this maniac? We stepped outside our gate to see who it was and — goodness me! The car was at our gate! A handsome young man got out and smiled at us. We knew then that this was the famous William himself! I was dying to ask him why he was going by so fast and he gave us the answer even before we did, "Couldn't find the house – that's why I drove up and down a couple of times to find the place." Well that was an answer – or rather half an answer! Anyway, introductions came around and we told William Bartholomeusz how good it was to meet him and he looked quite puzzled and then he said in a very firm tone, "My name is Wilhelm Balthazaar not William Bartholomeusz" – obviously thinking that we were all a loony bunch of people to get his name so wrong. Of course, we never divulged that his beloved Lorni was the one who had given us this name! So being a loyal and supportive family we bore the brunt of misnaming him! ☺ I immediately – and very politely excused myself and rushed back to my room holding onto my mouth so my giggles wouldn't be heard! I was relieved when I got back to the scene to see everyone chatting and laughing – so I too joined in. We were getting to know about his family and his school days – he was an old Trinitian which met my father's approval even though he usually favoured only the Royalists ha! Wilhelm left after a sumptuous dinner prepared by you-know-who!! Looking back, I don't know whether we had got the name mixed up due to the crackly 'trunk' calls we used to make to London! Anyway, all went off well – once again we saw him at the gate and yes, he did take off not with the crashing speed we had seen earlier but at a slow and very controlled pace! Maybe our influence had calmed him down!

Lorni came back from the UK a few months later and soon they planned to be married. His parents who lived in Kandy came down to visit and once again our families met and had dinner at our place. The wedding kept us really excited and busy. Our dear friend the super dressmaker Barney Labrooy did not only Lorni's bridal dress but also all our dresses! I was one of the bridesmaids and my cousin Ione Bartholomeusz was the other. Wilhelm's close planter friends Manilal Abeywardena and 'Phan' Dias were the best-men. Tiny second cousins Robert Peterson, and Tania Ephraims were the page boy and flower girl. All of us had very special outfits designed for us and we had to have several 'fit-ons' before the big day! Finally! The day arrived and we helped to decorate the Methodist Church at Colpetty where the service was being held. That evening at 5.30 my sister walked down the aisle with my dad and the rest of the bridal entourage followed them at a leisurely pace! It was a moving service and we had a reception at our house at Milagiriya Avenue. Barney was kind enough to open up her area of the house which gave us sufficient space to accommodate the guests. In those days weddings were not as elaborate as they are now. We did our own flower arrangements and most of the catering. Receptions were not as large and complex as they are today. Many relatives and friends attended and we had some lovely music on the radiogram and even had some dancing to liven up the evening! My sister, now Mrs Balthazaar, left with her husband on their honeymoon! We knew that they were now heading for their own future and they left for Houpe Estate, Kahawatte, where Wilhelm was working as a Senior Planter. Suddenly our house seemed so empty. No more did I have a sister to share the bedroom with. A sense of loneliness seeped into me and I just sat looking around at my room which didn't have her lovely jewellery and make up kits on the dressing table. I opened her almirah and it was empty. Well, another part of my life had emerged and I knew I had to face it with strength and determination.

Within a few months the La Brooy family decided to migrate to Australia and were planning to sell our house so we were compelled to find another place. Ironically at the same time my mother's sister – Aunty Dona and Uncle Leslie Campbell and their family, who lived in a house located in Dr R. L. Spittel's housing scheme at Dehiwala, were also going to Australia and we were fortunate to be able to move there. My uncle Eldie (my mother's brother) who was a widower and had no immediate family, lived with them, and he continued to stay with us when we moved in. Having lived at Milagiriya Ave for almost eight years the house became a part of our family – the bedrooms, the front verandah, sitting room, dining room – the back garden with the trees and the tiny front garden with floral plants were all cleared. Empty. Silent. Even our doggie Kim stayed quiet. The days of chatter and laughter and music and barking had all melted down into the past.

1962 – SRI SARANANKARA ROAD DEHIWALA

Around April 1962 when I was almost 18 years old we moved to Sri Saranankara Road, Dehiwala. There was a canal on one side of the road in front of our house and we lived on the opposite side of this – the land side. This house was smaller than the one at Milagiriya Avenue, so we had to make several adjustments and after the endless tidying up we finally settled down in our new abode. My Uncle Eldie continued to stay with us. We had a lovely little garden with a small lawn in front and lots of flowering plants which I enjoyed looking after.

My uncle's helper William stayed with us too – he used to drive my uncle's car when he was free from his daily morning job at a small kade nearby and stayed over at night at our place. He was usually back at home at around 2pm. He was always willing to help us out. On some weekends William would go to his village but when he was with us, he would clean up the garden and tidy the house. He would also bring us vegetables when we needed them. He slept in a room set up in the backyard and used the well for bathing and had his own toilet – so he was quite happy being here!

The banks that edged the canal were mainly occupied by the 'Dhoby' families, who used the canal as a washing source for their work. My dad however wanted all his clothes washed at home so I was the local 'dhoby'! No washing machines at that time. We had a well in our backyard and I had to draw buckets and buckets of water to do the washing! This became too tedious for me to handle! So, we got William to install a large cement sink with taps, adjoining our back verandah where I could wash our clothes and also wash our kitchenware, crockery and other tableware, and he built another sink to replace the tiny broken one we had just outside our kitchen. So, life became much more comfortable!

William was an excellent worker so I asked to help us tidy up our garden. The backyard was a grassy uneven area which became very muddy during the rainy weather as the rain water would flood this area, so we would not be able to step outside to put our clothes out to dry or for William to get to the well at the end of the garden! We decided to cement the whole area and gradient the level towards the end of the garden so that the water could flow down and enter the drain which was located near the well. He also put a *takarang* roof over the well which made it easy for him to have his baths during the rainy season and also on the side where we could dry our washed clothes! The walkway to the house from the front gate was also just a mushy sandy uneven roadway so this was also cemented and we could walk our way into the house without taking all the sand and mud on our feet! This was where my dad parked his Hillman Minx. The entrance on the other side where uncle Eldie parked his car was also cemented and proved to be easy access for him. The changes worked out very well – not only did they look so much neater but were much more practical and made our day to day life much easier!

We often visited Lorni and Wilhelm and enjoyed our stays at Houpe Estate, Kahawatte. They occupied a beautiful house and had a lovely garden and we had the opportunity to relax and enjoy ourselves! At Sri Saranankara Road we had caring neighbours and made lots of friends around our place and my dad used to take us to visit relatives – so it wasn't too bad. But after some time, I felt that our current location was not very convenient for me to get around to the areas of Colombo I was familiar with.

However, our happy environment was broken when sometime around August that year my Mother had a stroke and was in hospital for a few weeks. Then she was brought home. It was unbelievable to see her in this condition now – she couldn't walk, had lost her memory and could barely speak. It broke our hearts to see this once very active person just seated silently on a chair unable to move. She found it difficult to eat and I had to make her 'soft' food which I fed her during her mealtimes. There were no blenders or food processors at the time and I had to literally puree her food with a fork and spoon. Those were very hard and sad days for us. My dad felt very depressed to see my mum in this condition which meant that most of the time I had to handle things on my own. At nineteen years old I found these challenges difficult to deal with. It became a very trying time for all of us. We were so used to my mum attending to all the household needs that without her it was a formidable task for us to manage all this by ourselves. Although William did help with the cleaning on weekends, I found that looking after my mum, washing the clothes, doing the cooking and seeing to all the daily needs cast a heavy burden on me. However, we continued with our lives and with the passage of time I made up my mind to really take myself in hand and do something for myself. My sister and brother-in-law were always there to support us and often visited us.

We were blessed with caring friends Kamala and Frank Samaraweera and Charmaine and Annesley Philip and also many close relatives who visited regularly to help us with our needs for my mother. Also, our wonderful neighbours – particularly Conrad and Rita Hatch and Rita's sister and family willingly offered to supply our meals – lunch and dinner – which was a great relief for me. So, I only had to see to breakfast and our doggie Kim's food of course! I became a close friend of one of my neighbour's relatives, Rani, who later on helped me get a job at the office she worked in – and is still very much in contact with me.

My sister was a most wonderful source of strength and support through all these hard times. She would come down regularly from the estate to help out. She asked us to come over to the estate for Christmas and we decided we should do this – maybe my mum would feel happier with the family around her and my dad certainly needed a break – and so did I. Our neighbours saw to the needs of my uncle and our doggie Kim while we were away for the two weeks planned.

Christmas went by very well but on New Year's Day we noticed that my mum had developed a cough and was finding it difficult to breathe. Wilhelm brought a doctor he knew who examined her and said that she had a lung infection which had led to pneumonia. We arranged to take her to the nearest hospital but while waiting for the ambulance she took her last breath. This happened on January 2nd 1963. It was incredibly hard to imagine that my beloved mother had left us – that we would never see her again. My world had turned upside down and the realities of what had taken place just staggered me. Later I realised that my sister Lorni and her husband Wilhelm had organised all the funeral arrangements in Colombo. They stayed a few days with us after the funeral and when they left we felt so sad and bereft. My sister came down the following week and helped me clear all my mum's things – from her clothes to her other personal items. Her bed now lay empty and no longer was the chair in the sitting room filled with her presence. Even though I was absolutely grief stricken at her loss, I was always grateful that she didn't have to suffer for too long.

My dad went into deep depression after my mum died and he would lie on his bed the whole day and even coming to the table to have his meals became a big issue. I would have to remind him to have a shower – see that he had sufficient soap, toothpaste and towels. After a few months our little Cocker-Spaniel Kim who was almost 14 years old passed away. My heart was now broken as he was such a loveable pet and I felt that another member of my family had left us.

I took some time to get over all these sad issues in my life but also realised that I could not go on in this way and had to decide on some definite plans for the future. I was determined that I should face up to reality and do something. A friend gave me the name of a lady down Dickman's Road – Miss Rodgers – who conducted Secretarial Classes – shorthand, typing and how to write official letters for a Commercial Company. Getting to Dickman's Road was a bit of a tricky situation for me! I had to walk down Sri Saranankara Road then cross over on a bridge to a road which led to the Galle Road and then take a bus to Dickman's Road. Sounded quite easy – not too far either. BUT ... the grave issue was that the bridge that went over the canal was one made of wooden planks with chains holding the sides. The risky part was that most of the side chains were broken and many of the wooden planks were cracked and some were even missing! So, at certain parts of the bridge I had to jump to the next plank hanging onto a broken rail! There were times that I looked down and – gosh – there was the canal way down below my feet – if I missed my step I would fall right through! I did this for a few weeks but was always very stressed out and didn't do well at my classes. Then, I decided to take a longer route and managed to work out the correct direction! This route took a bit more walking and was more time consuming – but I felt so much safer! I began to enjoy the walk – passed lots of lovely little shops on the way that I would stop by and look – only look, not buy!! Meanwhile I was enjoying my classes and practised at home with my shorthand and soon reached the required levels by the teacher.

However, I felt that I was getting nowhere living where we did – at that time in the 1960s it was quite far away from my old familiar surroundings. My former school friends did keep in touch with me but it was difficult for them to travel so far from their homes. I do recall very well how Corinna Gauder visited me every week – she lived in Mount Lavinia and used to drive a car so she very kindly used to come over and take me out for an icecream! But I really was becoming despondent of my own lifestyle and was determined to move on to a level which would give me confidence and hope for my future. Finally, I managed to persuade my dad to shift towards a more convenient locality.

Fortunately, my neighbours had some relatives who stayed in an annex attached to a large house at Charlemont Road, Wellawatte. They were planning to vacate the place as they had decided to emigrate to Australia. The owner of the house was Mr Gordon

Austin who was the Managing Director of Rowlands Ltd. – a very high position for a Sri Lankan at that time. They mentioned to him that we were interested in renting their place and Mr Austin very kindly agreed to meet us. My dad's spirits perked up when I told him this – of course he had heard of Mr Austin and Rowlands was one of the best known commercial companies at the time! In addition, the location sounded perfect! So, dad and I met Mr Austin in his office the following week. He was very pleasant and took to us immediately and told us we could have the annex by the end of the following month. We got back home ready to make yet another change in our lives. We had to clear plenty of stuff from our present house as the place we were moving to was much smaller but nicely set out and conveniently located.

Our one problem was what would happen to my uncle Eldie when we left. Fortunately, my cousin Wendy offered to have my uncle – (her uncle as well - her dad's brother) – and William stay at their place. We were ever so grateful to them.

My dad's mood changed completely now that we were planning to go to Charlemont Road. Firstly, he took an instant liking to the Austins – and so did I. Also, the location was perfect for us – just off the Galle Road – Savoy Cinema at the top of the road, lots of shops around the corner – close to Frances Road where my aunt Queenie (my dad's late brother's wife) lived. My dad's sister Queenie died in 1964 and now her wonderful 'adopted' helper Dinah who had been with for many years continued to stay there, and also Tony the doggie. There was also my cousin Rita and her little daughter Loretta – so it was a house full of relatives just around the corner! At Kinross Avenue my cousin Margot and her husband Murad and son Shane lived. At Mary's Road were more relatives – the Bartholomeusz family – Aunty Esme, Uncle Carl and their children (my cousins!) Allister, Carol, Myrna, Ione and Heidi! We were surrounded by family members which made it very comfortable and secure for us!

So now began the preparations for the big move! We knew we had to cut down on a lot of our possessions and kept only the necessary items because the annex was much smaller than our present place.

My dad began clearing all his 'badus' with great vim and vigour! We had to cut down by more than half as there was plenty of furniture, crockery and other knick-knacks – and of course books! I suddenly saw a fire burning in the backyard – which was a cemented area – all his papers – so he said – but sadly he had burnt many photographs and letters relating to his and my mum's family. The flames were rising – I screamed – "Why are you doing this? All those lovely pictures and letters!" But there it was – all turning to ash. I dashed back to his room and picked up a bunch of papers and photos which had fallen on the floor – and these are the few which I have today! My sister Lorni came down especially to help us clear up and pack – and we told her to take whatever she wanted! Daddy gave all the leftover furniture – all made of teak mind you – to the dhoby community who lived on the banks in front of our house for which they were immensely grateful! Ajit Wijewardena – one of our old family friends – packed his car with our precious collection of books! We hired a van to move the larger items. And finally, we moved to our next location!

1964 – NO: 10 CHARLEMONT ROAD, COLOMBO 6

I was almost 20 when I moved here! The Austin annex was a small area but at that time in our lives a smaller place suited us fine. There was a sitting room, two bedrooms, one bathroom and a dining room with a tiny area which we used as a kitchen where we had a two-burner gas cooker and a small fridge. We also had a little garden in front and also at the back. Once at Charlemont Road, I made friends with Uncle Gordon and Auntie Julie Austin who were very kind and caring people. The Austins were a lovely family and we felt very comfortable and secure living in a part of their house. We shared a main entrance gate and would sometimes see them going in or out of their house. We also shared a common garden at the back which we used as an area to dry out our washed clothes. So, I would often chat in the garden while doing this! Their daughter Fae – was a young school girl at the time – she became friends with me and remains so to this day! Although Fae was much younger than I was, she became a close friend and as she grew older would often invite me to join her and her friends to some of their parties and get togethers – and even on some family trips out of Colombo. Real fun times! I also got back to visiting all my cousins nearby and catching up with school friends with whom I had lost touch over the past years. Next door to us was a mansion of a house where Stanley and Sheila Van Starrex and their kids lived – also the Furlongs whose daughters Sonia and Deirdre became my friends.

My dad came back to his old self again and actually took on some temporary work at the Health Ministry (where he was employed earlier) – and he began to visit the YMCA (his father was the founder President of the YMCA in Ceylon in June 1882) and regularly meet up with friends and do some administrative work there as well. These were all on a temporary basis so he wasn't compelled to go every day. The main thing was that he kept himself occupied and was quite happy. I loved strolling along the Galle Road at Wellawatte – so fascinating – lots of shops to explore and full of life and chatter!

In 1964 Lorni and Wilhelm were at Glenlyon Estate, Maskeliya and we were overjoyed to hear that my sister was expecting a baby! I couldn't believe that I was to be an aunt, and my dad was thrilled at the thought of being a grandfather! Our minds were split in two – happy and sad that my mother wasn't there to share our joy. On 19th September 1964 Michele Simone Balthazaar was born! We couldn't wait to go and see her! I well recall my dad and I going to the Fort Railway Station and taking a late-night train to Hatton and we reached Hatton early the next morning. Wilhelm sent a car to the station to pick us up and my dad insisted we go straight to the hospital to see the baby girl. I told him it was too early in the morning and we hadn't even had a shower and was it safe to visit a new born baby in this condition? But my dad was determined to see his granddaughter so he told the driver to go straight to the Hatton Nursing Home! This Nursing Home was run especially for the foreigners who lived in that area – mostly planters and their families of course. Michele was the first non-British baby to be born at this Nursing Home! Over the next few days we kept visiting them in the Nursing Home and when they returned home we spent a few, but truly unforgettable, days with them at Glenlyon before we got back to Colombo! On October 6th 1966 my sister had a son – named him Andre Wilhelm – it was such great fun for me to have a nephew – and of course for my dad to have a grandson!

Unfortunately, my dad and I were both hit by some serious medical problems. I developed appendicitis and had to have surgery. Quite scary for me – first time I ever had surgery!! After the operation my dad was in a daze – how were we going to manage when I got back home? My friend Siva (from George Steuarts) stayed close to the Nursing Home I was in and I will never forget how she would visit me every day – in the morning on her way to work and then again in the evening after office! As always, my sister came down and stayed with us for a few days and when I was feeling better went back to the estate! My aunt Queenie and cousin Margot sent our food every day and Auntie Julie gave us breakfast – so our meals were all sorted out! I will never forget how Auntie Julie came over every evening to help me have a safe shower and also sent the girl who worked for them to come over and sweep and dust our place. The kindness of family and friends was astounding! In a couple of weeks, I was fit enough to get back to the office – a few days a week at the start and then slowly back to my normal routine!

Not long afterwards, my dad suffered from an abdominal problem – hernia – which also had to be surgically treated. It was an emergency situation and late one evening he complained of a very severe pain in his abdomen and I was compelled to rush him to the hospital. He went into immediate surgery. The Chief Surgeon (can't remember his name) in charge was very impressed that I had brought the patient by myself and spoke very kindly to me. The anaesthetist was working on my dad – soon he was ready for surgery. Then the chief surgeon came out and said to me – "Have you ever seen a surgery take place?"

I stood up – "Ah no – I haven't – I…"

"Would you like to see a surgery being done?"

"Er – yes – why?" I replied, taking this as a joke!

"Ok then come inside – chance in a lifetime – and observe this" –with one nod of his head the assistant came out and put a gown on me, covered my face and put gloves on my hands.

"What's all this?"

"Dress for the theatre. Remember no talking – step into the theatre and stand here," he pointed his finger to a spot just next to him.

I just stood – still – silent – could hardly breathe. What in the world was happening?

"Now see this –he pointed to my dad's abdomen. This is where I have to cut." The nurse handed the scalpel and he made a deep cut – ooo – there was blood coming out – I stepped back. Couldn't see this – after all this was my father and the blood was pouring out.

"Come closer – don't move – don't talk – just keep your eyes on what I am doing and listen carefully to me."

He explained every detail of the surgery – I just stood but didn't hear most of it – felt dizzy –thought I was going to faint! I left the surgery and the doctor patted me on my shoulder –

"Consider yourself a lucky girl – not many people have actually seen a surgical procedure. Bring your dad to see me in two weeks." He smiled and I left in a daze – had I actually witnessed my dad's intestines being cut and sewn up? Oh gosh – can't be.

I was quite impressed that the surgical team were all very friendly and polite to me. After the surgery was over they got me to remove the gown, mask and gloves and then asked me in which college I was in London and how many more years did I have to complete my medical degree! What? I just smiled and left the room immediately. I had to stay over at the hospital that night and managed to go home the next morning to have a shower and change of clothes. I called the office and told them I wouldn't be able to come to work because of this situation and they were very understanding and told me to come when I was able to.

The next problem was how to deal with my dad's recovery? I had to go to work – there was no one at home. Fortunately, my sister and husband came down to Colombo when my dad was about to leave the hospital. Wilhelm had to be in Colombo for some weeks as he was involved in some work with the Head Office of the Tea Companies. They were staying temporarily at my cousin Eric & Bunty Peterson's house down Peterson Lane (which was quite close to Charlemont Road) and immediately asked dad and me to come over to their place. It was a very comfortable setting – so I was able to go to the office and also step in almost every day to check on our place at Charlemont Road. As always, Auntie Julie was there to help me so I had nothing really to worry about!

My dad loved telling all his visitors about his surgery – for the first visitors he told them how the doctor had removed six inches of his intestine – after two weeks his story grew to the doctor removing two feet – then three feet – and by the end of the next week his entire intestine was out! The visitors would be aghast – "So you have no intestines at all? Gosh that's terrible. How sad we are for you." Eyes edged with tears.

I chuckled – "No – the Doctor removed only about six or eight inches of intestine – not the whole thing Dad!" – "How do *you* know what the doctor did at the surgery?"

"Er – because – er – because I was there."

"What? How could you have been there? You're not a doctor or nurse or even an attendant?"

"No – er – the surgeon invited me to come in and observe the surgery – thought it would be a great opportunity for me to actually see an operation being done."

Silence. My dad did ask the surgeon when he went for his check-up and of course the doctor smilingly acknowledged this! Silence again. When he came back home he said – "Ah so now you can do the next surgery on me okay!"

After a lapse of about three or four weeks my dad had recovered well enough for us to return to Charlemont Road and get back to our normal routine again! To my great relief my sister would come regularly to see how we were doing! Another hurdle cleared☺.

My story will not be complete without mentioning the crazy happenings at Charlemont Road!

The Austins had a dog called Patch who was an absolute madcap! He would run around the garden catching various lizards and little animals and the weirdest thing was that he would jump on the lines in the garden where our clothes were being dried, and bring all the clothes down and scatter them all over. When my dad returned from office one evening, he found his clothes scattered all over on Charlemont Road and also on the front lawn of the house! When I returned from work shortly thereafter, he was picking up clothes from the ground and I wondered what had come over him!!! Can't imagine what those walking on the road thought☺. Then I heard the story – and gosh I even found some of my clothes in the bushes and on the chairs on the verandah of their house!

Auntie Julie was shocked to see this mess and apologised profusely to us! She helped us to pick up the stuff and we had to get back home and yes, I had to re-wash everything!!! Uncle Gordon very kindly built a light trellis doorway in the garden just in front of the entrance to our annex and another one on the side so that naughty Patch couldn't throw our clothes out again! So, the side garden and my room became the drying area for clothes!!!

Patch also used to run into the Wellawatte canal which bordered the rear part of the garden. Many people used to fish along this canal and boats kept going up and down all the time. We could hear them shouting and talking but couldn't see them. The Austins placed some boulders at the edge and grew some trees and bushes in that part of the garden which prevented anyone from seeing our house from the canal. But these didn't keep Patch from dashing down into the canal and getting back soaking wet with a fish in his mouth! This happened a couple of times and then two of the fishermen jumped with him over the line of boulders which edged the land and came into the garden and then into the rear of the house. Aunty Julie, Uncle Gordon and Fae had a tough time consoling the men and gave them a good sum of money to resolve the issue! After this Uncle Gordon got a huge barbed wire fence fixed to edge this boundary and Patch was unable to escape on that side! So now he was limited to a small area and I really don't know what he did to keep himself occupied. A year or so later Patch died and was buried in the garden of his roaming days. It was a sad day for all of us.

Some months later Fae who loved animals – decided she needed a new pet. To our great surprise she came home one day with a baby monkey in her hands. This was it – the new pet! She named him Monkey – he was very sweet – large eyes blinking and yes there was a smile on his face. She looked after Monkey like a human baby – so he slept in her room in a little cot and she would give him his baths in the bathroom she used and then feed him with a little milk bottle and a few biscuits and bread – so yes there was a baby in the house!

Auntie Julie planned to have some friends over to tea and I offered to help. Ladies came walking in and seated themselves on the verandah and inside the sitting room. I poured out the drinks and brought them out for them – and all the tasty short eats and cake on the serving dishes! Then Fae walked out – still in her bathrobe and with baby Monkey wrapped up in a towel and cradled in her arms. All you could see was Monkey's face. Everyone rushed to see the baby – they peered and some of them frowned. Monkey rolled his big eyes and made a twitter folding mouth up and down. The ladies went back to their seats – all silent.

Auntie Julie was at the dining table again telling her maid to refill the dishes with the eats. I walked back biting my lips – the chuckles bursting inside me. Not long after this most of the guests decided to get back home so there was another rumble of feet and chatter before they left. It was time for me to leave too. Where was Fae and Monkey? Inside her room – putting him to sleep? When I finally left, Auntie thanked me profusely for all my help and gave me a whole pile of eats to take back! No signs of Fae – her door was shut – couldn't disturb the baby what!!

Baby monkey grew slowly but surely and soon he was climbing all the trees in the garden and jumping on the roof and yes, he also crept into our annex and pulled some stuff off the kitchen shelf! He took a fancy to the clothes on the line – we could put them out now that Patch had gone – but this wasn't working out because now 'Monkey' monkey was picking up the clothes from the line and not putting them on the ground as Patch did – he was taking them up the roof and also the trees – so we could see our clothes hanging on the mango tree and laid out on the roof! He would sit up there and try them on – yes even underwear over his head – oh my gosh, how were we to stop this??

We had a *takarang* cover put over our little garden so that the monkey couldn't get in and this is where we dried our clothes and could open our front door and windows without a problem. The back door of course had to be opened and shut very carefully!

Then came further catastrophe! Uncle Gordon very methodically kept all his medicines in a box by the dining table. Well Monkey was kept mostly within the house – Fae used to keep him in her room but when she was out of the house this was totally impossible! He used to run out of the room, dash into the garden and then jump on the roof. One day I heard Auntie Julie shouting out and the girl who worked there screaming and I went out immediately to see what had happened. There they were standing on the lawn looking up and shouting – "Come down, come down at once!" I looked up – Monkey was on the top of the roof seated down with a box and he was fiddling inside and pulling out little packets of – oh my gosh – Uncle Gordon's medicines! He was flinging the pills and potions all over the roof and some bottles came crashing to the ground. Then he sat quietly, took a packet and upset it into his hand – oh pills pills pills – Auntie Julie shouted "Those are Gordon's pills – don't touch those!" Monkey gazed down at her, cupped his hand out, put pills, rolled his head back and in they went! Pandemonium followed – all of us shouting and Monkey running all over the roof. Some neighbours hearing the noise also looked over the wall. Finally, he came down and looked totally dazed – maybe the reaction of the pills? He went into his room and we put him to sleep in his little bed that lay beside Fae's! A few days later Fae realised that she couldn't really bring up a monkey and fortunately we had a neighbour who did have a couple of monkeys – she had large caged areas with trees growing inside – so she was quite happy to take the not-so-little monkey to add to her family! Such a relief for us! I remember walking down with Fae to hand over the monkey – she was very silent on the way back home and went straight into her room and closed the door. I did understand and so did Auntie Julie. The little friend in her room was no longer there.

I'll never forget the time when Fae asked me to join her and her parents to go on a trip to Polonnaruwa for the weekend. I was thrilled to go on a trip after such a long time! We stayed at the Polonnaruwa Resthouse which stood on the border of the lake. The tour guides at the hotel advised us that at some places in the lake the water took a very deep dip and near the edges by the hotel it was mostly shallow. They also warned us that there were crocodiles sometimes in the lake and to be very aware of this as they could be quite dangerous! Fae was an excellent swimmer but I wasn't – so when she decided to go for a swim and asked me to join – I did – but I stuck to the rocky edge of the lake and enjoyed having a dip in shallow water. I enjoyed just mooching around in the water and could see Fae in the distance doing an energetic swim, arms and legs moving with great rhythm and pace! The shout came from behind me and when I turned around the guide was there telling me that crocodiles had been spotted and to come out immediately. They also kept shouting through a loudspeaker "Crocodiles spotted – very dangerous – come out of the lake immediately!" But Fae continued with her la-la swim – happily going along – meanwhile I was on the edge screaming my head off. Uncle Gordon and Aunty Julie also came out with all this noise and there was such a loud rumpus going on – and yes, we could see some crocodiles moving silently popping their heads up and down and – Fae still enjoying her swim. Finally, a life-guard came, leapt into the lake and swam at furious pace towards Fae and she looked startled and of course more startled when he gave her the news and she too could spot the crocs making their way across the water! She swam at top speed and reached the edge in just a few seconds. Thank God she was an excellent swimmer!! Otherwise, the crocs would have had a sumptuous lunch what!! We were all so relieved to have her safely back with us – but I do remember she was blasted by her dad!

After a few years Fae decided to go to Australia and I really missed having her around. But she still remains one of my dearest friends. Some of her friends were now my friends as well. Michele Leembruggen was one of them and she still is a very close friend of mine.

GEORGE STEUART DAYS!
Now I faced another chapter in my life. It was very convenient for me to go for my secretarial classes at Miss Rodgers, Dickmans Road – I looked forward to

doing this. Soon I had completed the Secretarial Course – with very good results! I managed to get a job at a local mercantile company in the Fort (with the help of Rani) and after about a year I was fortunate to be employed as a stenographer to the late Mr Scott Dircksz, the Personnel Manager at George Steuart & Co. Ltd., which was one of the largest British run agencies for the tea industry in Sri Lanka at that time. Scott Dircksz was appointed as a Director shortly thereafter and I was assigned to the foreign owned estates department located upstairs – these were the Office Administrators of the foreign owned estates. The ground floor held the offices of Directors, their Secretaries and other staff. Further down towards the rear of the building were the staff lunch rooms/toilets and lockers – women and men separately. The first floor accommodated some of the staff members and the switchboard for our telephone operator – no mobile phones then! There was a mezzanine floor between the first and the second floors which held the Accounts department. On the second floor was the Estates department – where I worked. The office for the management of the local Tea Estates and the Tea Tasting division headed by Tony Peiries, was located in a building nearby (across the road) and had their own staff.

In our section the Managers each had either one or two stenos – who of course sat at their desks nearby with their typewriters ready, waiting to be called upon when work commenced! The Managers I recall were St. Elmo Gunasekera, Ajit Goonetilleke, Sunil Gunawardena (for whom I worked), Michael Loos, David Labrooy, Rex Herman and K. S. Peiries. Among the other staff members the names I remember are Siva Sinniah– our very efficient Telephone Operator, Joyce Dissanayake (Secretary to the Directors) and Pam Weerakoon (Asst. Secretary to the Directors) – Jeanne Mendis, Gary de Silva, and later Asanka de Mel in the Accounts Department and in our department there were Preethi Perera, Venetia Rutnam (called Vaness by us), Jackie Moldrich, Audrey Bastiansz, Jennifer Shervonne, Barbara Spittel, Francesca Leembroogen (we called her Fran), Melanie Sansoni, Dennis Berenger, Dudley de Silva. Other departments had Leslie Vandersay, Helen, Heather, Carol, Yolande Rabot, and MaryAnne. When Siva left to go to England we had Deirdre Furlong and later Valerie Blake at the Telephone Operator's post. I still have the wedding gifts given to me by Dennis – a lovely stand holder for small saucepans etc., and a large metal rack – for my kitchen! I still keep in contact with many of my old friends at George Steuarts and we thoroughly enjoy reminiscing about the 'good old days!'

At the entrance an official 'Doorman' stood, clad in white sarong and long shirt to meet the visitors and clients to the office. There was John who constantly kept cleaning the brass covering which topped the bannisters along the stairways – no elevators what? There were photographs of some British Royalty hung along a small wall at the bottom of the stairway and John had to see that they were clean and kept straight on the wall! We had to pass this wall when we went down for our tea/lunch breaks, and would just tick our finger against a photo on the wall which made it slide slightly out of line! Later we would see John checking the photos and re-straightening them! The Directors of GS were all foreigners at that time (until Scott was appointed!) One of the Managers (on our floor) felt it was his duty to stand up each time he got a call from a foreign person! So, a joker in our midst ☺ would call him from a phone downstairs and speak with a very British accent – which he was incredibly clever at doing – and mention the name of a Director. He would tell a few of us when he was going to do this so we would be watching eagerly!

The phone rings. The Manager would pick it up and immediately rock up from his chair with a 'Yes Sir,' response.

The voice said 'Come down immediately I want to speak to you.'

Manager would dash down and we could hear his footsteps beating along the wooden stairway!

We would be waiting at our desks for the return. Five minutes – ten minutes – what? Ah, then we could hear the *plonk plonk plonk* – the coming up – he would storm to his desk – "Bloody shits those buggers –!" his secretary would gently ask "Why Sir, – what happened?" "After calling me all the way down he said he never called – does he think I'm mad or something? All of you heard me talking to him so how can he say he didn't call. He's totally mad, that's what he is."

We would remain silent, not even daring to look at one another. Our joker walked into the room carrying a file – alert and silent. Then left without even a glance.

This Manager also had the habit of removing his shoes when he was seated at his desk and another Joker (No. 2) picked them up and put them into the waste bin. Then signalled to Joker No. 1 to make the usual call. The same procedure followed, but when the Manager tried to find his shoes to go downstairs he couldn't find them! He shouted – "My shoes! My shoes! – where the hell are my shoes?" Everyone stopped working and wondered what this was all about. His secretary spoke, "What's happened to your shoes Sir?"

"They are missing – can't you see that I'm searching for them!"

We felt we had to help and joined in the search! So, all work was stopped and almost everyone was looking here and there – for the missing shoes! Then happily we discovered them in the waste bin – but Joker 2 grabbed them and just slid them under the Manager's table – "Here Sir – they're here."

"How could they have been there – I looked there no – dammit!"

Calm prevailed and he pulled on his shoes and dashed down the stairway. Came back with the usual reaction. When was this going to stop??

At that time the Fort was mainly a high-level shopping area and some of the best shops were located there. The names of Cargills, Millers – down York Street, the

Colombo Apothecaries located at Lloyd's building, book shops such as K. V. G de Silvas at the YMBA Building, and H. W. Cave & Co. at Gaffoor Building. My sister's former school friend Pauline Mack ran a beautiful Hair Dressing Salon at Apothecaries and I used to go to her regularly for my haircuts! Chatham Street was based close to our office so it was easy for us to dash down to the Pagoda Café to have a quick ice cream and while walking along would drop in at the shops down the road! Shopping at the Pettah – located a short distance away from our office, was also quite an experience but I would do this on a Saturday because during our lunch break there was no time to roam through the streets of Pettah and get back to the office in time! The shop I remember is Titus Stores down Main Street – also recall 1st Cross Street! There were separate places where vegetables and dry rations were sold. I was totally mesmerised by the numerous shops with their large rolls of fabric, boxes of costume jewellery, handbags – and the millions of knick-knacks laid out on shopping stalls set up on the pavements lining the road! I would literally spend hours wandering around these places!

   I used to join a group of my George Steuart friends – and also sometimes Fae and her friends – and often on Saturdays we used to go to the Coconut Grove at the Galle Face Hotel to listen and dance to the tunes of the fabulous band – Mignonne and the Jetliners where we did the rock and roll and jived till early morning!!! There was also the Burgher Recreation Club at Havelock Road, the Ceylonese Rugby & Football

Club, and the Colombo Hockey and Football Club – popular places to watch the matches and then stay over for some eats! Among the other nightclubs whose names I remember were the Mascarilla, Akase Kade, the Blue Leopard at the Grand Oriental Hotel and The Little Hut. The names of musical bands and singers I recall were Ishan Bahar, Harold Seneviratne, Sam the Man and the Gaylords, Gabo and the Breakaways, and Dalreen Suby and the Fireflies. There must have been many more but these are all I can remember. They used to keep us dancing and singing through the evening.

I reached the age of 21 in 1965 while I was working at George Steuarts. My sister and her husband were now on Dewalakande Estate, Dehiowita. They wanted me to spend my birthday with them and sent their car to take my dad and me there. My friends insisted I should have a celebration for this special occasion! So, my sister very kindly offered to have a lunch for them. The GS crowd extended from eight to ten to twelve and then to twenty! They were travelling from Colombo in a van and those with cars brought some of them. I shall never forget how as the numbers had increased the cook at my sister's estate was becoming quite stressed and we had to chip in and help with the preparation of the lunch! Finally, at around 12.30pm the vehicles all drew up and yes, there was a crowd! They loved looking around the house and the beautiful garden. I recall how my friend Jeanne Mendis came down the stairway – carrying my niece Michele who was just under a year old – waving to us as she walked down! We were thoroughly nervous that Jeanne would trip down and drop the little girl – and we all breathed a huge sigh of relief when they finally reached the ground floor! Anyway, the lunch was absolutely super and the cook had turned out several desserts plus a lovely birthday cake for me! So, everyone had a fantastic time and left late that evening leaving us quite exhausted – but really very happy! Wonderful for me to have family and friends like them!

Charlemont Road was very convenient for us. Some relatives lived nearby although many of them had emigrated to Australia. My Aunt Queenie was still at Frances Road, and my cousin Margot and Murad Uduman and son Shane at Kinross Avenue. This was very fortunate for me as Aunt Queenie used to supply our lunch – to my Dad at Charlemont Road, and mine was sent by a 'lunch-boy' who came to my workplace – George Steuarts, during the week. On weekends the lunch-boy took a break, so we used to go to my aunt's and get our really tasty lunches! My dad used to walk over to Margot's place and collect the wonderful dinners she made for us!

Also, often Shane and I would meet up in the evenings and go out to have an icecream! Shane and I are still close friends.

We used a different English language then! Said Hello instead of Hi, Cheerio instead of Bye, Okey Dokes instead of ok, telephone you instead of call, film and film stars not movie stars, and went to the pictures instead of movies, there were bathrooms and lavatories and also toilets no washrooms!! These are just a few I can remember!

I spent some happy years at George Steuarts and made several friends, many who are still in contact with me. I look back at the great times at GS&CO – dashing down to the Pagoda Restaurant down Chatham Street every day for ice cream. It was on one of these runs that my colleague at GS – Pam Pullenayagam (nee Weerakoon), who was also an actress and took part in several plays at the Lionel Wendt, was with us, and suddenly saw a small group of guys walking on the other side of the street – she gave a shout (acting style:)) 'Julius Sagamore' and believe it or not one of the guys turned around and waved to her! We were stunned! "What was that? Is that guy's name Julius Sagamore?" "Yes – we are both in a play together – that's his stage name silly!"

Then I remembered Bernard Shaw's play *The Millionairess* where Pam was playing the main role! Julius Sagamore was there! Didn't we scream and laugh! So almost every day we did come across Julius – who strangely was a lawyer at Julius & Creasy – weird what?

Soon Julius Sagamore came over and spoke to Pam and of course she had to introduce him to all of us☺ Sriyantha Senaratna – also called Simon – sounds familiar what?

My life changed again when I met the love of my life and we got married and are still together after 52 years! ☺

Our two children have grown up to be very responsible adults and are married with children – my daughter

Sonali is married to Dinesh Sellamuttu and they have a son Akash who's now 17 years and my son Dimitri and Sarah have a daughter Audrey who will be 17 early next year and a son Isaak who will be 14. They live in the US, but we are in constant touch with one another – thanks to modern technology! Fortunately, at the time of writing this, it has been a couple of years since Sonali, Dinesh and Akash moved back from abroad to Colombo. Last year Dimitri's daughter Audrey was permitted a gap year from school – so she came down and lived with Sonali and Dinesh, and attended the same school as Akash and were in the same class! Needless to say, we all enjoyed having her here!

So – my life so far has been a memorable one – not too many achievements I'm afraid, but I have learnt to deal with the ups and downs of the reality of life. My faith in the Good Lord has always helped me to get through all the hard times that came my way and I will always remember that He is by my side at all times. So, life goes on – getting old has its own problems but here again I know that Jesus is always there for me

ACKNOWLEDGEMENTS

My family always wanted me to write about memories of my childhood and growing up days. They listened to me relating the stories and insisted that I put it down in a book! So here it is!

I am ever grateful to my beloved husband Simon, for all his love and support in my writing these stories! Also, my loving family – Sonali, Dinesh and Akash, and Dimitri, Sarah, Audrey and Isaak who are always there for me. I cannot forget my pets – sweet doggie Jenna, tortoise Barney, fish in the pond and birds on the trees – who gave me 'break-times' to relax!

Also thanks very much to my friend Jill McDonald who gave me some very valuable and constructive advice at the beginning of my writing endeavor!

Always grateful to my caring sister Lorni – relatives and devoted friends who were constantly feeding me with their stories in my life and pressing me to get the book done!

And last but not least – my most sincere gratitude to Ameena who very kindly analyzed my work and agreed to publish this book.

My eternal gratitude to the Lord for always being there for me.

About the Author

Anthea Senaratna lives in Colombo with her husband Sriyantha (also called Simon!) – who is a lawyer, and her family of pets – which include one very sweet black Cocker-Spaniel Jenna, Barney the Tortoise, and the number of birds, bees and butterflies, squirrels and thalagoyas who wander through the garden!

She studied at schools in Trincomalee and Kurunegala and finally wound up at Methodist College. She has a Diploma in English from the University of London (External Programme).

She writes articles, short stories and poems and has been published both locally and abroad and is a member of two writers' groups – The Wadiya Group and the English Writers' Collective. She wrote travel articles for the Lanka Monthly Digest for several years. She has been a regular writer to the *Noel* Magazine published each Christmas! Some of her prose was published in the Iowa 100 Words Magazine, 1997, and she was on the final shortlist of the Commonwealth Short Story Competition in 1997. She has published three books of short stories – *Dancing with the Dogs – and other short stories*, *The Mango Tree – stories & sketches* which was shortlisted for the Gratiaen Prize 2008, and *A Flash of Red and other stories*.

Her interest in Rotary was brought in by Simon – a very senior and dedicated Rotarian, and she is very happy to be a member and participate in the activities of the Rotary

Club of Colombo North – especially the Inter-Schools' Shakespeare Drama Competition! She is a member of the Women's Auxiliary Association of the Colombo YMCA, the Dutch Burgher Union, and the Animals Welfare and Protection Association. She is also involved in several charitable organisations and finds it very rewarding to help those in need.

Her interests include reading, writing, music, art, animals, cooking and gardening, and loves travelling to familiar and also new destinations.

She is a dedicated Christian and enjoys participating in the church activities, and is most grateful to the Lord for all the blessings He has placed upon her.